SECOND EDITION

TOUCHSTONE

STUDENT'S BOOK

1B

MICHAEL McCARTHY

JEANNE McCARTEN

HELEN SANDIFORD

CAMBRIDGE
UNIVERSITY PRESS

CAMBRIDGE
UNIVERSITY PRESS

32 Avenue of the Americas, New York, NY 10013-2473, USA

Cambridge University Press is part of the University of Cambridge.

It furthers the University's mission by disseminating knowledge in the pursuit of education, learning and research at the highest international levels of excellence.

www.cambridge.org
Information on this title: www.cambridge.org/9781107613669

First published 2005
Second Edition 2014

Printed in Hong Kong, China, by Golden Cup Printing Company Limited

A catalog record for this publication is available from the British Library.

ISBN 978-1-107-67987-0 Student's Book
ISBN 978-1-107-62792-5 Student's Book A
ISBN 978-1-107-65345-0 Student's Book B
ISBN 978-1-107-63933-1 Workbook
ISBN 978-1-107-67071-6 Workbook A
ISBN 978-1-107-69125-4 Workbook B
ISBN 978-1-107-68330-3 Full Contact
ISBN 978-1-107-66769-3 Full Contact A
ISBN 978-1-107-61366-9 Full Contact B
ISBN 978-1-107-64223-2 Teacher's Edition with Assessment Audio CD/CD-ROM
ISBN 978-1-107-61414-7 Class Audio CDs (4)

Additional resources for this publication at www.cambridge.org/touchstone2

Touchstone Second Edition has benefited from extensive development research. The authors and publishers would like to extend their thanks to the following reviewers and consultants for their valuable insights and suggestions:

Ana Lúcia da Costa Maia de Almeida and Mônica da Costa Monteiro de Souza from **IBEU**, Rio de Janeiro, Brazil; Andreza Cristiane Melo do Lago from **Magic English School,** Manaus, Brazil; Magaly Mendes Lemos from **ICBEU**, São José dos Campos, Brazil; Maria Lucia Zaorob, São Paulo, Brazil; Patricia McKay Aronis from **CEL LEP**, São Paulo, Brazil; Carlos Gontow, São Paulo, Brazil; Christiane Augusto Gomes da Silva from **Colégio Visconde de Porto Seguro,** São Paulo, Brazil; Silvana Fontana from **Lord's Idiomas**, São Paulo, Brazil; Alexander Fabiano Morishigue from **Speed Up Idiomas**, Jales, Brazil; Elisabeth Blom from **Casa Thomas Jefferson**, Brasília, Brazil; Michelle Dear from **International Academy of English**, Toronto, ON, Canada; Walter Duarte Marin, Laura Hurtado Portela, Jorge Quiroga, and Ricardo Suarez, from **Centro Colombo Americano**, Bogotá, Colombia; Jhon Jairo Castaneda Macias from **Praxis English Academy**, Bucaramanga, Colombia; Gloria Liliana Moreno Vizcaino from **Universidad Santo Tomas**, Bogotá, Colombia; Elizabeth Ortiz from **Copol English Institute (COPEI)**, Guayaquil, Ecuador; Henry Foster from **Kyoto Tachibana University**, Kyoto, Japan; Steven Kirk from **Tokyo University**, Tokyo, Japan; J. Lake from **Fukuoka Woman's University**, Fukuoka, Japan; Etsuko Yoshida from **Mie University**, Mie, Japan; B. Bricklin Zeff from **Hokkai Gakuen University**, Hokkaido, Japan; Ziad Abu-Hamatteh from **Al-Balqa' Applied University**, Al-Salt, Jordan; Roxana Pérez Flores from **Universidad Autonoma de Coahuila Language Center**, Saltillo, Mexico; Kim Alejandro Soriano Jimenez from **Universidad Politecnica de Altamira**, Altamira, Mexico; Tere Calderon Rosas from **Universidad Autonoma Metropolitana Campus Iztapalapa**, Mexico City, Mexico; Lilia Bondareva, Polina Ermakova, and Elena Frumina, from **National Research Technical University MISiS**, Moscow, Russia; Dianne C. Ellis from **Kyung Hee University**, Gyeonggi-do, South Korea; Jason M. Ham and Victoria Jo from **Institute of Foreign Language Education, Catholic University of Korea**, Gyeonggi-do, South Korea; Shaun Manning from **Hankuk University of Foreign Studies**, Seoul, South Korea; Natalie Renton from **Busan National University of Education**, Busan, South Korea; Chris Soutter from **Busan University of Foreign Studies**, Busan, South Korea; Andrew Cook from **Dong A University**, Busan, South Korea; Raymond Wowk from **Daejin University**, Gyeonggi-do, South Korea; Ming-Hui Hsieh and Jessie Huang from **National Central University**, Zhongli, Taiwan; Kim Phillips from **Chinese Culture University**, Taipei, Taiwan; Alex Shih from **China University of Technology**, Taipei Ta-Liao Township, Taiwan; Porntip Bodeepongse from **Thaksin University**, Songkhla, Thailand; Nattaya Puakpong and Pannathon Sangarun from **Suranaree University of Technology**, Nakhon Ratchasima, Thailand; Barbara Richards, Gloria Stewner-Manzanares, and Caroline Thompson, from **Montgomery College**, Rockville, MD, USA; Kerry Vrabel from **Gateway Community College**, Phoenix, AZ, USA.

Touchstone Second Edition authors and publishers would also like to thank the following individuals and institutions who have provided excellent feedback and support on **Touchstone Blended:**

Gordon Lewis, Vice President, Laureate Languages and Chris Johnson, Director, Laureate English Programs, Latin America from **Laureate International Universities; Universidad de las Americas**, Santiago, Chile; **University of Victoria**, Paris, France; **Universidad Technólogica Centroamericana**, Honduras; **Institut Universitaire de Casablanca**, Morocco; **Universidad Peruana de Ciencias Aplicadas**, Lima, Peru; **CIBERTEC**, Peru; **National Research Technical University (MiSIS)**, Moscow, Russia; **Institut Obert de Catalunya (IOC)**, Barcelona, Spain; Sedat Çilingir, Burcu Tezcan Ünal, and Didem Mutçalıoğlu from **İstanbul Bilgi Üniversitesi**, Istanbul, Turkey.

Touchstone Second Edition authors and publishers would also like to thank the following contributors to **Touchstone Second Edition:**

Sue Aldcorn, Frances Amrani, Deborah Gordon, Lisa Hutchins, Nancy Jordan, Steven Kirk, Genevieve Kocienda, Geraldine Mark, Julianna Nielsen, Kathryn O'Dell, Ellen Shaw, Kristin Sherman, Luis Silva Susa, Mary Vaughn, Kerry S. Vrabel, and Eric Zuarino.

Authors' Acknowledgments

The authors would like to thank all the Cambridge University Press staff and freelancers who were involved in the creation of *Touchstone Second Edition*. In addition, they would like to acknowledge a huge debt of gratitude that they owe to two people: Mary Vaughn, for her role in creating *Touchstone First Edition* and for being a constant source of wisdom ever since, and Bryan Fletcher, who also had the vision that has led to the success of *Touchstone Blended Learning*.

Helen Sandiford would like to thank her family for their love and support, especially her husband Bryan.

The author team would also like to thank each other, for the joy of working together, sharing the same professional dedication, and for the mutual support and friendship.

Finally, the authors would like to thank our dear friend Alejandro Martinez, Global Training Manager, who sadly passed away in 2012. He is greatly missed by all who had the pleasure to work with him. Alex was a huge supporter of *Touchstone* and everyone is deeply grateful to him for his contribution to its success.

Touchstone Level 1B Contents and learning outcomes

	Learning outcomes	Language		
		Grammar	Vocabulary	Pronunciation
Unit 7 Out and about pages 65–74	• Describe the weather • Talk about ongoing activities with the present continuous • Talk about sports and exercise • Ask about current activities using the present continuous • Ask follow-up questions to keep a conversation going • React to news with *That's great, That's too bad*, etc. • Read an article about exergaming • Write an article about exercise using imperatives	• Present continuous statements, *yes-no* questions, short answers, and information questions • Imperatives ***Extra practice***	• Seasons • Weather • Sports and exercise with *play, do,* and *go* • Common responses to good and bad news	***Speaking naturally*** • Stress and intonation in questions ***Sounds right*** • Sounds like *ou* in *four* or *or* in *word*
Unit 8 Shopping pages 75–84	• Talk about clothes • Say what you *like to, want to, need to,* and *have to* do • Talk about accessories • Ask about prices using *How much . . . ?, this, that, these,* and *those* • Take time to think using *Uh, Let's see,* etc. • Use *Uh-huh* and *Oh* in responses • Read a review of a shopping mall • Write a review of a store using *because*	• *Like to, want to, need to,* and *have to* • Questions with *How much . . . ?; this, these; that, those* ***Extra practice***	• Clothing and accessories • Jewelry • Colors • Shopping expressions • Prices • "Time to think" expressions • "Conversation sounds"	***Speaking naturally*** • *Want to* and *have to* ***Sounds right*** • Sounds like *a* in *hat*
Unit 9 A wide world pages 85–94	• Give sightseeing information with *can* and *can't* • Talk about international foods, places, and people • Say what languages you can speak • Explain words using *kind of* and *kind of like* • Use *like* to give examples • Read a travel website • Write a paragraph for a travel website	• *Can* and *can't* for ability and possibility ***Extra practice***	• Sightseeing activities • Countries • Regions • Languages • Nationalities	***Speaking naturally*** • *Can* and *can't* ***Sounds right*** • Sounds like *sh* in *she* or *ch* in *child*
Checkpoint Units 7–9 pages 95–96				
Unit 10 Busy lives pages 97–106	• Talk about last night using simple past regular verbs • Describe the past week using simple past irregular verbs • Ask simple past *yes-no* questions • Respond to news with *Good for you,* etc. • Say *You did?* to show surprise or interest • Read about a blogger's week • Write a blog about your week, using *after, before, when,* and *then*	• Simple past statements, *yes-no* questions, and short answers ***Extra practice***	• Simple past irregular verbs • Time expressions for the past • Fixed expressions	***Speaking naturally*** • *-ed* endings ***Sounds right*** • Sounds like *oo* in *looked, ou* in *bought, o* in *spoke,* or *e* in *left*
Unit 11 Looking back pages 107–116	• Describe past experiences • Ask and answer questions using the past of *be* • Talk about vacations • Talk about activities with *go* and *get* expressions • Show interest by answering and then asking a similar question • Use *Anyway* to change the topic or end a conversation • Read a funny magazine story • Write a story using punctuation for conversations	• Simple past of *be* in statements, *yes-no* questions, and short answers • Simple past information questions ***Extra practice***	• Adjectives to describe feelings • Expressions with *go* and *get*	***Speaking naturally*** • Stress and intonation in questions and answers ***Sounds right*** • Which vowel sound is different?
Unit 12 Fabulous food pages 117–126	• Talk about eating habits using countable and uncountable nouns, *How much,* and *How many* • Talk about food • Make offers using *Would you like . . .* and *some* or *any* • Use *or something* and *or anything* in lists • End *yes-no* questions with *or . . . ?* to be less direct • Read a restaurant guide • Write a restaurant review	• Countable and uncountable nouns • *How much . . . ?* and *How many . . . ?* • *Would you like (to) . . . ?* and *I'd like (to) . . .* • *Some* and *any* • *A lot of, much,* and *many* ***Extra practice***	• Foods and food groups • Expressions for eating habits • Adjectives to describe restaurants	***Speaking naturally*** • *Would you . . . ?* ***Sounds right*** • Syllable stress
Checkpoint Units 10–12 pages 127–128				

Interaction	Skills				Self study
Conversation strategies	Listening	Reading	Writing	Free talk	Vocabulary notebook
• Ask follow-up questions to keep a conversation going • React with expressions like *That's great!* and *That's too bad*	***That's great!*** • Listen to people tell you their news and choose a good follow-up question to ask them ***Do you enjoy it?*** • Listen to people talk about exercises they like	***Exergaming: Give it a try!*** • Read an article about exergaming	***An article for a health magazine*** • Write a short article giving advice about exercise • Use imperatives to give advice	***Find out about your classmates*** • Class activity: Learn interesting facts about classmates	***Who's doing what?*** • Write new words in true sentences
• Take time to think using *Uh, Um, Well, Let's see,* and *Let me think* • Use "sounds" like *Uh-huh* to show you are listening, and *Oh* to show your feelings	***I'll take it.*** • Listen to conversations in a store, and write the prices of items and which items people buy ***Favorite places to shop*** • Listen to someone talk about shopping, and identify shopping preferences and habits	***The Dubai Mall: Shopping, Entertainment, Lifestyle*** • Read a review of a mall	***Favorite places to shop*** • Write a review for your favorite store • Link ideas with *because* to give reasons	***How do you like to dress?*** • Group work: Compare ideas about shopping and clothing	***Nice outfit!*** • Label pictures with new vocabulary
• Explain words using *a kind of, kind of like,* and *like* • Use *like* to give examples	***International dishes*** • Listen to a person talking about international foods, and identify the foods she likes ***What language is it from?*** • Listen to a conversation, and identify the origin and meaning of words	***The Travel Guide*** • Read a travel website	***An online travel guide*** • Write a paragraph for a travel guide • Commas in lists	***Where in the world?*** • Pair work: Discuss where to do various things in the world	***People and nations*** • Group new vocabulary in two ways

Checkpoint Units 7–9   pages 95–96

• Respond with expressions like *Good luck, You poor thing,* etc. • Use *You did?* to show that you are interested or surprised, or that you are listening	***Good week? Bad week?*** • Listen to people talk about their week and respond ***Guess what I did!*** • Listen to voice mail messages about what people did	***She said yes!!!*** • Read Martin's Blog entry	***A great day*** • Write a blog entry • Order events with *before, after, when,* and *then*	***Yesterday*** • Pair work: Look at a picture and list what you remember	***Ways with verbs*** • Write down information about new verbs
• Show interest by answering a question and then asking a similar one • Use *Anyway* to change the topic or end a conversation	***Weekend fun*** • Listen to conversations about peoples' weekends, and identify main topics and details ***Funny stories*** • Listen to two stories, identify the details, and then predict the endings	***How embarrassing!*** • Read a funny magazine story	***He said, she said*** • Complete a funny story • Use punctuation to show direct quotations or speech	***Guess where I went on vacation.*** • Group work: Guess classmates' dream vacations	***Past experiences*** • Use a time chart to log new vocabulary
• Use *or something* and *or anything* to make a general statement • End *yes-no* questions with *or . . . ?* to be less direct	***If you want my advice . . .*** • Listen to people talking about lunch, and identify what they want; then react to statements ***Do you recommend it?*** • Listen to someone tell a friend about a restaurant and identify important details about it	***Restaurant guide*** • Restaurant descriptions and recommendations	***Do you recommend it?*** • Write a restaurant review • Use adjectives to describe restaurants	***Plan a picnic*** • Group work: Plan a picnic menu and make a shopping list	***I love to eat!*** • Group vocabulary by things you like and don't like

Checkpoint Units 10–12   pages 127–128

v

Getting help

What's the word for "_____" in English?

How do you spell "_____"?

What does "_____" mean?

I'm sorry. Can you repeat that, please?

Can you say that again, please?

Can you explain the activity again, please?

Working with a partner

I'm ready. Are you ready?

No. Just a minute.

You go first.

OK. I'll go first.

What do you have for number 1?

I have . . .

Do you want to be A or B?

I'll be A. You can be B.

Let's do the activity again.

OK. Let's change roles.

That's it. We're finished.

What do we do next?

Can I read your paragraph?

Sure. Here you go.

Out and about

✓ Can Do! **In this unit, you learn how to . . .**

Lesson A
- Describe the weather
- Talk about ongoing activities with the present continuous

Lesson B
- Talk about sports and exercise
- Ask about current activities using the present continuous

Lesson C
- Ask follow-up questions to keep a conversation going
- React to news with *That's great, That's too bad*, etc.

Lesson D
- Read an article about exergaming
- Write an article about exercise using imperatives

Before you begin . . .

Match the pictures and seasons. Which seasons do you have? What's the weather usually like in each season?

2 spring   5 fall   3 rainy season

1 summer   4 winter   6 dry season

It's hot and humid.
It's warm and sunny.
It's cool. It's often cloudy.
It's windy. It's cold.
It rains.
It snows.

It's 2:30 p.m. on Saturday, and Anita is at work in San Francisco. She usually relaxes on Saturdays, but she's working this weekend. Right now she's taking a break and listening to her voice mail. All her friends are having fun!

MARCH
21ST
SATURDAY

Saturday, 8:45 a.m.
Hi, Anita. This is Yoko. I'm calling from a ski resort in Lake Tahoe. Lisa and I are skiing today. It's so beautiful here, and there's lots of snow. It's snowing right now. I'm sorry you're working. What's the weather like in San Francisco? Give me a call. Bye.

Saturday, 10:20 a.m.
Hi, it's Bill. Listen, Marcos and I are at the beach in Santa Cruz. Come and join us! Don't worry – we're not swimming. It's too cold and cloudy. See you.

Saturday, 11:15 a.m.
Hey, Anita. This is Nathan. I'm in San Jose with Katie and Rob. They're playing tennis, and I'm watching. It's nice and sunny. I hope it's not raining there. Call me! Bye.

1 Getting started

A Look at the pictures. Where is Anita? Where are her friends?

B 🔊 2.24 Listen. What's the weather like in each place?

Figure it out **C** What are Anita and her friends doing? Circle the correct words.

1. Anita usually relaxes on Saturdays, but today **she works / she's working**!
2. Yoko says, "Lisa and I **am / are** skiing today. **It snows / It's snowing** here right now."
3. Bill says, "Marcos and I are at the beach . . . **we're not / we don't** swimming. It's too cold!"
4. Nathan says, "I'm in San Jose with Katie and Rob. **They / They're** playing tennis."

2 Grammar   Present continuous statements ◀)) 2.25

Extra practice p. 145

Use the present continuous to talk about right now or today.

I'm	calling	from home.
You're	working	today.
She's	skiing	with a friend.
He's — (not) —	having	fun.
It's	raining	right now.
We're	swimming	in the ocean.
They're	playing	tennis.

The contractions *isn't* and *aren't* often follow nouns:

Marcos **isn't** working.
Marcos and Bill **aren't** swimming.

Spelling

work	▶	wor**king**
swim	▶	swim**ming**
have	▶	ha**ving**

> ☰ **In conversation**
>
> In the present continuous, people usually use *'s not* and *'re not* after pronouns. People don't usually say *we aren't, they aren't, he isn't*, etc.

A ◀)) 2.26 Complete Anita's other voice mail messages. Then listen and check.

1
Saturday, 11:45 a.m.
Hi, Anita. This is Andrea. I _'m calling_ (call) from the mall. I'm in a café with Chris. We _having_ (have) lunch right now. Chris _Isn't stay_ (not stay) long. He _is shopping_ (shop) for a new computer. So let's meet. Give me a call. See you!

2
Saturday, 1:30 p.m.
Hey, Anita, it's me, John. I'm at Andrew's house. We _'re watching_ (watch) the baseball game. The Giants _are not playing_ (not play) very well. And now it _is raining_ (rain). Um, let's meet for dinner. Call me on my cell. Bye.

3
Saturday, 2:00 p.m.
Hi. Where are you? I hope you _aren't work_ (not work). Listen, Chloe _isn't working_ (not work) today, and I _'m not doing_ (not do) anything special. You know, I _'m cleaning_ (clean) the house, and Chloe _is doing_ (do) laundry. So come over around 5:00, and have an early dinner. Call me.

B Prepare a voice mail message for a friend. Then take turns saying your messages to the class. Who's having the most fun?

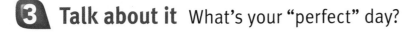

"Hi there. This is _____ .
I'm at _____ .
I'm _____ .
The weather is ____ Cool ____ it ___ rainy ___ ."

> ✕ **Common errors**
>
> Always use *be* with the present continuous:
> *It's raining.* (NOT ~~It raining.~~)

3 Talk about it   What's your "perfect" day?

A Imagine you are having a perfect day. Think of answers to the questions below.

▶ Where are you?
▶ What's the weather like?
▶ Who are you with?
▶ What are you doing?

"On my perfect day, I'm at the beach. It's very hot and I'm sleeping. I'm . . ."

About you **B** **Class activity** Go around the class, and tell your classmates about your perfect day. Can you find anyone with the same ideas?

1 Building vocabulary

A 🔊 **2.27** Listen and repeat the sentences.

They're playing . . .

basketball

football

volleyball

They're doing . . .

aerobics

weight training

karate

They're . . .

bowling

running

biking

Word sort **B** Complete the chart with the activities above and add your own ideas. Compare with a partner.

I often . . .	Sometimes I . . .	I never . . .
go running.	do aerobics.	play soccer.
go biking	do weight training	play basketball
volleyball		do karate
		go basketball

> **ℹ Note**
> I'm bowling / running / biking right now.
> I go bowling / running / biking every week.

📓 **Vocabulary notebook** p. 74

2 Building language

A 🔊 **2.28** Listen. Is Carl studying hard this semester? What is he doing right now?
Practice the conversation.

Dad Hi, Carl. It's me. How's it going?

Carl Oh, hi, Dad. Everything's great.

Dad So are you studying for your exams?

Carl Oh, yeah. I'm working very hard this semester.

Dad Good. So what are you doing right now? Are you studying?

Carl Uh, Dad, right now I'm watching a baseball game.

Dad Baseball? . . . Uh, who's playing?

Carl The Yankees and the Red Sox.

Dad Really? Uh, Carl, . . . let's talk again in two hours.

Carl OK, Dad. Enjoy the game!

Dad You too. But please try and study for your exams!

Figure it out **B** Underline the questions in the conversation above. What do you notice about the word order?

3 Grammar Present continuous questions ◀)) 2.29

Extra practice p. 145

Information questions
What **are** you **doing** these days?
What **is** Carl **watching** on TV?
Who **'s** he **talking** to right now?

Information questions with *who* as subject
Who **'s playing?** (The Yankees.)
Who **'s watching** the game? (Carl.)

Yes-no questions and short answers

Are you	**studying** hard?	Yes, I **am**.	No, I**'m not**.
Is Carl	**watching** the game?	Yes, he **is**.	No, he**'s not**.
Are the Yankees	**playing?**	Yes, they **are**.	No, they**'re not**.

You can use the present continuous for activities "around now."
I'm working very hard this semester.

Time expressions

right now
today
this morning
this week
this month
this year
this semester
this season
these days

A Complete the questions with the present continuous.

1. What ___are___ you ___doing___ (do) for exercise these days?
2. ___Are___ you ___running___ (run)? ___Are___ you ___swimming___ (swim)?
3. ___Are___ you ___getting___ (get) enough exercise?
4. ___Is___ your best friend ___taking___ (take) an exercise class?
5. Who ___'s exercising___ (exercise) more – you or your best friend?
6. ___Are___ you ___watching___ (watch) any special sporting events on TV this week?
7. _____ your friends ___playing___ (play) on any sports teams this year? How about you?
8. How ___is___ your favorite sports team ___doing___ (do) this season? Who on the team ___are___ ___playing___ (play) well?

About you **B Pair work** Ask and answer the questions. Give your own answers.

A *What are you doing for exercise these days?*
B *Well, I'm taking a weights class at the gym this month.*

4 Speaking naturally Stress and intonation in questions

How often do you go to the gym?   *Are you going a lot these days?*

A ◀)) 2.30 Listen and repeat the questions. Notice how the words *gym* and *lot* are stressed. Notice how the voice falls on *gym* and rises on *lot*.

B ◀)) 2.31 Listen. Repeat these pairs of questions.

1. How often do you play **sports**? Are you playing a **lot** these days?
2. When do you **study**? Are you studying **hard** right now?
3. How are your **classes** going this year? I mean, are they going **well**?

About you **C Pair work** Ask and answer the questions above. Give your own answers.

(((· Sounds right p. 138

1 Conversation strategy Asking follow-up questions

A Look at the picture of Tina, Kate, and Ray. What are they doing?

B 🔊 2.32 Listen. What is Kate doing in Laguna Beach this week?

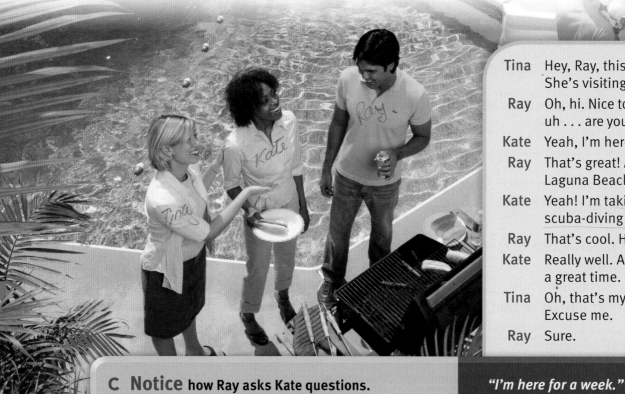

Tina	Hey, Ray, this is my friend Kate. She's visiting from Chicago.
Ray	Oh, hi. Nice to meet you. So, uh . . . are you here on vacation?
Kate	Yeah, I'm here for a week.
Ray	That's great! Are you enjoying Laguna Beach?
Kate	Yeah! I'm taking a scuba-diving course.
Ray	That's cool. How's it going?
Kate	Really well. And I'm having a great time.
Tina	Oh, that's my cell phone. Excuse me.
Ray	Sure.

C Notice how Ray asks Kate questions. He keeps the conversation going. Find examples in the conversation.

"I'm here for a week."
"That's great! Are you enjoying Laguna Beach?"

D 🔊 2.33 Complete the conversations with the follow-up questions. There is one extra question. Then listen and check your answers. Practice with a partner.

1. A You know, I'm taking a French class.
   B Really? _Are you enjoying it_
   A Yeah. It's going pretty well. I like it.
   B That's good. _Are you learning about the culture, too_
   A Yeah. It's interesting. So how about you? _Are you taking any interesting classes_

2. A I'm reading a couple of really good books.
   B Yeah? _What are you reading?_
   A Oh, a book by Suzanne Collins, and a book about music.
   B That's interesting. _So do you have an e-reader, too?_

Are you taking any interesting classes?

Are you enjoying it?

So do you have an e-reader?

Are you learning about the culture, too?

So where are you going? To clubs?

What are you reading?

2 Strategy plus *That's . . .*

You can use expressions with
That's . . . to react to news.

 In conversation

The top expressions for good news are:

*That's **good** / **great** / **nice** / **interesting** / **cool** / **wonderful**.*

The top expressions for bad news are:

*Oh, that's **too bad** / **terrible**.*

I'm here for a week.

That's great.

Complete the responses using an expression with *That's*. Then practice with a partner.

1. A I'm taking a yoga course this week. I'm really enjoying it.

   B Oh, _that's good_ .

2. A I'm feeling really tired. I'm not sleeping well and I'm not eating.

   B Really? _that's terrible_ .

3. A A friend of mine is studying sports science.

   B Really? _that's interested_ .

4. A My friends are on vacation this week. They're biking in the Alps.

   B Oh, _that's cool_ .

3 Listening and strategies *That's great!*

A 🔊 2.34 **Listen to six people tell you their news. Respond using an expression with *That's*. Then choose a good follow-up question. Write the letters *a* to *f*.**

1. That's _____ .   _c_
2. That's _____ .   _e_
3. That's _Terrible_ .   _f_
4. That's _____ .   _d_
5. That's _____ .   _a_
6. That's _nice_ .   _b_

a. So what are you reading right now?
b. Who's playing?
c. So what are you doing? I mean, are you making coffee?
d. It sounds interesting. Is it playing every day?
e. What's she doing all day? Is she blogging?
f. Why is he seeing her? Do you know?

B 🔊 2.34 **Listen again. Write one piece of information about each person's news.**

About
you **C** **Pair work** Take turns telling your partner some interesting news. Respond with *That's . . .* and ask follow-up questions.

A I'm playing on the school volleyball team this year.

B That's great. How's the team doing?

Free talk p. 133

1 Reading

A For which exercise activities do you do these things? Tell the class.

- have a personal trainer
- pay a fee
- buy special equipment
- get feedback on your progress

📖 **Reading tip**

Read the main headings first. They tell you what the article covers.

B Read the article. Why is exergaming a good idea?

EXERGAMING *Give it a try!*

College student Aaron Case plays tennis every day, even when it's raining – like today. But Aaron isn't getting wet. He's playing against a virtual tennis professional on his TV. These days, there are millions of "exergamers" like Aaron. They're skiing, playing golf, and doing karate in their own homes. Video exercise games are popular with <u>people of all ages</u>, and it's easy to see why.

▶ **The weather is never a problem.** Is it raining or snowing? Maybe it's hot and humid outside. Don't worry. Exercise indoors.

▶ **It's convenient.** Stay home and work out in front of your TV!

▶ **It's motivating.** Don't pay for an expensive personal trainer. With exergaming, you see your scores and get feedback on your progress.

▶ **There's variety.** Try something new. Exergames have everything from aerobics to yoga. There are a lot of different types of games, so you never get bored.

▶ **It's fun.** Work out with a friend, or play a game with a family member.

▶ **It's not expensive.** Forget about monthly gym fees. Just buy the basic equipment and a game, and after that, exergaming is free!

So, if you're looking for convenient, cheap, and fun ways to exercise, why not give exergaming a try?

C According to the article, are these sentences true or false? Check (✓) *True* (T) or *False* (F). Correct the false statements.

		T	F
1.	Aaron Case is playing tennis outdoors in the rain.	☐	☑
2.	Only young people enjoy exergaming.	☐	☑
3.	Some personal trainers are expensive.	☑	☐
4.	Exergamers don't get bored.	☑	☐
5.	You pay monthly fees for some games.	☐	☑
6.	The equipment for exergaming is free.	☐	☑

About you **D** **Pair work** Do you agree that exergaming is good exercise? Why or why not? Discuss with your partner.

2 Listening Do you enjoy it?

A Look at the pictures below. What are the people doing? Do you or your friends do these things?

B 🔊 2.35 Listen to four conversations. Number the pictures 1 to 4.

C 🔊 2.35 Listen again. Answer the questions in the chart.

	How often do the people do the activities?	What do they like about the activities?
1.		
2.	Every weekend	
3.	Every Saturday	
4.	Every day	Is convenient. Is free

About you **D** **Pair work** What do you think about the different activities above? Discuss the pros and cons.

3 Writing Get moving!

A Read the Help note and the article. Underline the verbs that are imperatives for advice.

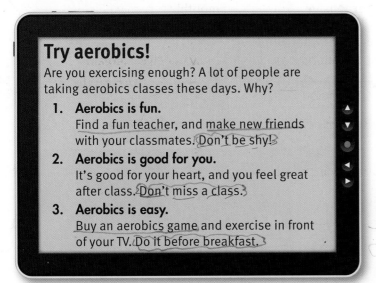

Try aerobics!

Are you exercising enough? A lot of people are taking aerobics classes these days. Why?

1. **Aerobics is fun.**
   Find a fun teacher, and make new friends with your classmates. Don't be shy!
2. **Aerobics is good for you.**
   It's good for your heart, and you feel great after class. Don't miss a class.
3. **Aerobics is easy.**
   Buy an aerobics game and exercise in front of your TV. Do it before breakfast.

🖊 Help note

Imperatives for advice

An imperative = verb
- *Find* a fun teacher.
- *Make* new friends.

A negative imperative = Don't + verb
- *Don't be* shy!
- *Don't miss* a class.

About you **B** Choose an exercise activity you enjoy. Write an article giving ideas and advice like the one above.

C **Pair work** Read a classmate's article. Ask questions to find out more information.

Vocabulary notebook / Who's doing what?

Learning tip *Writing true sentences*

To remember new vocabulary, use words in true sentences.

In conversation

It's cold outside!

In the U.S. and Canada, the top six weather expressions with *it's* are:

1. It's cold.
2. It's hot.
3. It's raining.
4. It's windy.
5. It's humid.
6. It's snowing.

People say *It's cold* 10 times more than *It's hot*.

1 Complete the sentences about the weather.

1. Right now it's ___cloudy___ outside.
2. At this time of year, it usually ___is cold___ .
3. In the summer, it's ___Hot___ .
4. In the winter, it's ___cold___ .
5. I like the weather when it's ___summer___ , but I don't like it when it's ___snowing___ .

2 Write the names of at least three people you know. Complete the chart with true sentences.

	Name	Where is he or she right now?	What is he or she doing right now?	What is he or she doing these days?
1	my brother Juan	He's at school.	He's studying math right now.	He's playing soccer and basketball.
2	Manny	He's at office	He's working	He's doing his weight training
3	Masca	She's at school	She's studying	she's playing volleyball
4	Yfon	He's in NJ	He's working	He's studying English
5	Mila	She's in Lima	She's working	She's going to running
6		She's at Home	She's eating breakfast	She's cooking

On your own

Take a minute this week, and look around you. What are people doing? Write six sentences.

He's snoring.

Now I can . . .

☑ I can . . .   ? I need to review how to . . .

- ☐ describe the weather.
- ☐ talk about sports and exercise.
- ☐ ask questions about what people are doing.
- ☐ keep a conversation going.
- ☐ react to good or bad news.
- ☐ listen and respond to people's news.
- ☐ understand people talking about their exercise routines.
- ☐ read an article about exergaming.
- ☐ write a short article giving advice about exercise.

Shopping

✓ Can Do! In this unit, you learn how to . . .

Lesson A
- Talk about clothes
- Say what you *like to*, *want to*, *need to*, and *have to* do

Lesson B
- Talk about accessories
- Ask about prices using *How much . . . ?*, *this*, *that*, *these*, and *those*

Lesson C
- Take time to think using *Uh*, *Let's see*, etc.
- Use *Uh-huh* and *Oh* in responses

Lesson D
- Read a review of a shopping mall
- Write a review of a store using *because*

1

2

3

4

Before you begin . . .

Look at the pictures. What are the people wearing? What are your classmates wearing? Use the words below.

- 2 pants and a top
- 1 a dress and high heels
- jeans
- a cardigan
- 4 a sweatshirt
- 3 a suit and tie
- sweatpants
- a T-shirt

What kinds of clothes do you like to wear?

Kyoko Takano, 16, high school student

Well, we don't have to wear uniforms at our school, so I like to wear pants, a T-shirt, and sneakers. So yeah, I'm lucky. My friend has to wear a uniform, and she hates it.

Emre Yilmaz, 27, accountant

I have to wear a suit and tie to work. After work, I just want to go home and put on jeans and an old sweater. You know, something comfortable.

Bethany Philips, 32, advertising executive

Well, my boss likes to wear designer clothes, so I need to look good, too. I usually wear a nice skirt or dressy pants with a silk blouse, and a jacket. Oh, and high heels.

 Getting started

A Look at the photos above. Who is wearing these things?

a jacket _Bethany_   a silk blouse _Bethany_   a skirt _Bethany_

sneakers _Kyoko_   a sweater _Emre_

B 🔊 2.36 Listen. Who wears casual clothes to school or work? Who wears formal clothes?

Figure it out **C** Circle the correct words. Use the interviews above to help you.

1. Emre says, "After work, I just **want** / **want to** put on jeans and an old sweater."
2. Kyoko says, "I like **to wear** / **wear** pants, a T-shirt, and sneakers."
3. Kyoko doesn't **have** / **have to** wear a uniform. She doesn't need to **wear** / **wearing** formal clothes.
4. Bethany's boss wears designer clothes, so Louisa **has to** / **has** look good, too.

About you **D** **Pair work** Are you like Kyoko, Emre, or Bethany? Tell a partner.

2 Grammar *Like to, want to, need to, have to* ◄)) 2.37

Extra practice p. 146

After the verbs *want* and *like*, you can use *to* + verb.

What do you **want to wear** tonight?
  I **want to wear** my new outfit.
  I don't **want to wear** my old dress.

What kinds of clothes does Bethany **like to wear** to work?
  She **likes to wear** designer clothes.
  She doesn't **like to wear** casual clothes to work.

Use *need to* + verb and *have to* + verb to talk about needs and rules.

What do you **need to buy**?
Do you **need to buy** new shoes?
  Yes, I do. I **need to get** some sneakers.

What does Emre **have to wear** to work?
Does he **have to wear** a suit?
  Yes, he does. He **has to wear** a suit and tie.

About you Complete the conversations. Practice with a partner. Then ask the questions again and give your own answers.

1. A What do you _like to wear_ (like / wear) at home in the evening?

    B I usually just _want to relax_ (want / relax). I _like to put on_ (like / put on) jeans.

2. A Do your friends _have to wear_ (have to / wear) a uniform to school or work?

    B No, they don't. My friend Jenna _has to look_ (have to / look) good for work.
      But she _doesn't have to wear_ (not have to / wear) a uniform.

3. A Do you _like to buy_ (like / buy) clothes online?
      Or do you _have to see_ (have to / see) things first?

    B No, I always _need to try on_ (need / try on) clothes.
      So I _don't like to shop_ (not like / shop) online.

4. A Are stores expensive here? I mean, do you _have to pay_ (have to / pay) a lot for jeans?

    B Well, there are expensive stores. But you _don't need_ (not need / shop) at those places.

> **✕ Common errors**
>
> Simple present short answers end with a form of *do*.
>
> *Do you like to wear jeans?*
> *No, I* ***don't****. (NOT No, I don't like.)*

3 Speaking naturally *Want to* and *have to*

"wanna"	*I **want to** buy some new clothes.*	"hafta"	*I **have to** buy some new clothes.*
	*What do you **want to** buy?*		*What do you **have to** buy?*

A ◄)) 2.38 Listen and repeat the sentences above. Notice the reduction of *want to* and *have to*.

B ◄)) 2.39 Now listen and repeat these questions.

1. Do you have to go shopping this week? . . . Where do you have to go?
2. Do you have to buy any new clothes? . . . What do you have to get?
3. Do you want to spend a lot of money? . . . How much do you want to spend?
4. Do you want to go to a designer store? . . . Which stores do you want to go to?

About you **C** **Pair work** Ask and answer the questions above. What do you and your partner have in common?

    A ***Do you have to go shopping this week?***
    B ***Yes, I have to go shopping on Saturday.***

Lesson B / Things to buy

1 Building vocabulary

A 🔊 2.40 Listen and say the words. Which items do you have? Which do you want to buy? Tell the class.

a baseball cap

a belt

a backpack

a briefcase

a purse

shoes and socks

a bracelet and a ring

a necklace and earrings

a coat and boots

a hat, a scarf, and gloves

Word sort **B** 🔊 2.41 Listen and say the names of the colors. What clothes and accessories do you have in these colors? Write them in the chart. Compare with a partner.

white	black	red	blue	brown	green	yellow	gray	pink	orange
coat	jeans briefcase boots shoes socks pants T-shirt	purse	snickeers	belt	bracelit ring	baseball cap	backpack	hat scarf gloves	

"I have three pairs of black jeans. I like to wear black."

earrings rings   purse

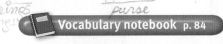
Vocabulary notebook p. 84

2 Building language

A 🔊 2.42 Listen. How much are the gloves and the scarf? Practice the conversation.

Salesperson Hello. Can I help you?
Stacy Uh, hi. How much are those gloves?
Salesperson These? They're really popular. They're $80.
Stacy Hmm. And what about that blue scarf? How much is that?
Salesperson This scarf is on sale. It's only $149.
Stacy A hundred and forty-nine dollars? OK, I have to think about it. Thanks anyway.

Figure it out **B** Circle the correct word in each sentence. Then practice with a partner.

1. A How much are **those** / **this** earrings?

   B **This** / **These**? They're $80.

2. A And the ring? How much is **that** / **those**?

   B **This** / **These** ring is on sale.

3 **Grammar** *How much . . . ?; this, these; that, those* 🔊 2.43

Extra practice p. 146

How much is it?
How much is **this** scarf?
How much is **this**?
  It's $49.99.

How much is **that** watch?
How much is **that**?
  It's $475.

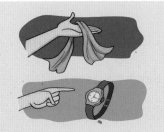

How much are they?
How much are **these** gloves?
How much are **these**?
  They're $125.

How much are **those** sunglasses?
How much are **those**?
  They're $50.

Saying prices

$125 = A hundred and twenty-five (dollars) $49.99 = Forty-nine dollars and ninety-nine cents
                                                        OR Forty-nine ninety-nine

In conversation

People also say *How much does it cost?* and *How much do they cost?* to talk about prices in general.

A Write questions with *How much . . . ?* and *this, that, these,* and *those.* Then practice with a partner.

1 How much are these green scarves?
   They're 39

It's 14.99

2 How much is that wine baseball cap?

It's 198

3 How much is this gray brief case?

 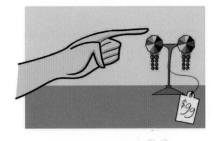 

They're $75

4 How much are those brown shoes?

They're $99

5 How much are those green earrings?

6 How much is this black coat?
   It's 975

B **Pair work** Take turns asking the questions above again. This time give your own prices.

About you **C** **Pair work** How much do you usually have to pay for the items above? Agree on an average price.

  A How much do nice scarves cost? About fifty dollars?
  B Maybe between fifty and seventy-five dollars.

1 Conversation strategy Taking time to think

A Look at the photo. What do you think Sarah wants to buy?

B 🔊 2.44 Listen. What does Sarah buy? Who is it for?

Clerk	Can I help you?
Sarah	Uh, yes. I'm looking for a bracelet.
Clerk	All right. Is it a gift?
Sarah	Uh-huh, it's a birthday present for my sister.
Clerk	OK. And um, how much do you want to spend?
Sarah	Well, let's see . . . about $30.
Clerk	Uh-huh. Well, we have these silver bracelets here.
Sarah	Oh, they're beautiful: Um, how much is this?
Clerk	Um, it's . . . let's see . . . it's $55.95.
Sarah	Oh. That's a lot. Let me think. . . . Well, it's perfect for me. OK. I'll take it. Now, I need something for my sister!

C Notice how Sarah and the clerk say *Uh, Um, Well, Let's see,* and *Let me think* when they need time to think. Find examples in the conversation.

> *"Um, how much do you want to spend?"*
> *"Well, let's see . . ."*

D 🔊 2.45 Listen. Complete the conversations with the expressions in the box. There is one extra. Then practice with a partner.

Well, um	Let's see	Let me think	Uh	Um

1. A Do you like to wear jewelry?

    B ___Let's see___ , I like to wear these rings and my watch. But that's it.

2. A What's your favorite store?

    B ___Let me think___ , I like to shop at the mall. There are a lot of good stores there.

3. A How much do you like to spend on birthday presents?

    B ___Well, um___ , I guess I spend about $15 or $20 on my friends.

4. A Where's a good place for electronics?

    B ___Um___ . . . . Well, I like to shop online. So I'm not really sure.

About you **E Pair work** Ask and answer the questions above. Give your own answers. Use the expressions in the box if you need time to think.

2 Strategy plus "Conversation sounds"

Uh-huh means *"Yes,"* *"That's right,"* or *"I'm listening."*

Oh shows you're surprised, happy, upset, or angry.

Is it a gift?

Uh-huh.

Let's see . . . it's $55.95.

Oh. That's a lot.

In conversation

Uh-huh and *Oh* are in the top 50 words.

🔊 **2.46** Complete the conversations using conversation sounds with the meanings given. Then listen and check. Practice with a partner.

1. A You have some money with you, right?

   B _____Uh-huh_____ (*yes*). I have about $30.

   A _____Oh_____ (*happy*) good. Can I borrow $10?

   B _____Oh_____ (*upset*), not again!

2. A I have about nine or ten credit cards.

   B _____Oh!_____ (*surprised*), that's a lot!

   A _____Uh-huh_____ (*yes*). But I never carry cash.

3. A I have to go shopping this weekend.

   B _____Uh-huh_____ (*I'm listening*).

   A Yeah. I want to buy a tablet.

   B _____Oh!_____ (*surprised*), cool!

3 Listening and strategies *I'll take it.*

A 🔊 **2.47** Listen to three conversations in a store. Write the price of each item.

① $199.95 $41.50

② $79.95 $74.95

③ $15.95 $

B 🔊 **2.47** Listen again. Circle the items the shoppers buy. Why do they choose these items? Write a reason for each item.

About you **C** **Pair work** Role-play the situation below. Then change roles.

Student A: You need to buy a gift for someone very special – your wife or husband, or a girlfriend or boyfriend. You don't have a lot of money to spend.

Student B: You're a clerk in a store. You need to sell something. Try to sell your customer something expensive!

A *Can I help you?*

B *Yes. I'm looking for a gift for my girlfriend.*

Learning tip *Labeling pictures*

To learn new vocabulary, you can label pictures in books, magazines, or catalogs.

In conversation

It's black and white!

Here are the top ten colors people talk about.

1. white	6. green
2. black	7. yellow
3. red	8. gray
4. blue	9. pink
5. brown	10. orange

1 Label the clothing and accessories in this picture.

- white necklace
- brown hat
- pink sweater
- white blouse
- Black belt
- Yellow purse
- gray skirt
- gray high heel
- white shirt
- red tie
- Watch
- brown Jacket
- the suit have two brown Jacket and black Pants
- black Pan
- orange socks
- black shoes
- gray briefcase
- green Umbrell

2 Find and label at least three pictures you like from a magazine or catalog.

 On your own

Go into a big clothing store. How many things can you name in English?

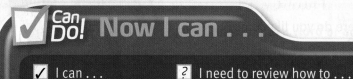

✓ Can Do! Now I can . . .

✓ I can . . .   ? I need to review how to . . .

- ☐ talk about clothes and accessories.
- ☐ say what I like, want, need, and have to do.
- ☐ ask for prices of things in stores.
- ☐ discuss my shopping habits.
- ☐ take time to think.

- ☐ show that I'm listening and show my feelings.
- ☐ understand conversations about prices.
- ☐ understand a conversation about shopping habits.
- ☐ read a review of a mall.
- ☐ write a review of a store.

A wide world

✓ Can Do! In this unit, you learn how to . . .

Lesson A
- Give sightseeing information with *can* and *can't*

Lesson B
- Talk about international foods, places, and people
- Say what languages you can speak

Lesson C
- Explain words using *kind of* and *kind of like*
- Use *like* to give examples

Lesson D
- Read a travel website
- Write a paragraph for a travel website

1. take tours of castles

2. see pyramids

3. take photos of famous bridges

4. walk around historic districts and look at statues

5. go to the tops of towers

6. visit palaces

Before you begin . . .

Do you like to go sightseeing? Check (✓) the activities above you like to do. What other things do you like to do when you visit other places?

5 Great things to do in New York

1. Go to Broadway, and see Times Square.

2. Take a ferry to see the Statue of Liberty.

3. Visit one of over 50 museums and buy some souvenirs.

4. Go to the top of the Empire State Building and get a view of the city.

5. Take a walk through Central Park.

HOTEL

Emma	Oh, no. It's raining! What can you do in New York on a day like this?
Ethan	Oh, come on. You can do a million things. We can take a ferry to the Statue of Liberty.
Emma	A ferry – in this weather?
Ethan	Well, . . . we can go to the top of the Empire State Building.
Emma	But you can't see anything in the rain.
Ethan	Yeah, you're right. I know – let's go to a Broadway show. There are shows on Wednesday afternoons.
Emma	OK. It's a deal. But first can we buy an umbrella?
Ethan	Sure we can. Look, there's a store over there.

1 Getting started

A Look at the page from a guidebook. Which activities are good when it's sunny? Which are good when it's raining?

B 🔊 2.49 Listen. What do Emma and Ethan decide to do? Practice the conversation.

Figure it out **C** Circle the correct words. Use the conversation above to help you.

1. We can **to go / go to** the Statue of Liberty.

2. You can't **see / seeing** the views because it's raining.

3. What **we can / can we** do in New York on a rainy day?

4. **Do we / Can we** buy an umbrella?

About you **D** **Pair work** What are some things you can do in New York City? Take turns giving ideas.

"You can take a walk through Central Park."

86

2 Grammar *Can* and *can't* for possibility 🔊 2.50

Extra practice p. 147

Use *can* to talk about things that are possible. Use *can't* for things that are not possible.

| I You He She We They | can can't | take a ferry. see a show. go to a museum. |

What **can** you do in New York?
You **can** do a million things.

Can we buy an umbrella?
Yes, we **can**.
No, we **can't**.

💬 **In conversation**

You is the most common word before *can*. *You* often means "people in general."

You can't take pictures. = It's not possible to take pictures.

A Match the questions and answers about New York City. Then practice with a partner.

1. Can you visit a historic neighborhood? ___d___

2. What kinds of museums can you go to? ___e___

3. Can you take a bus tour? ___f___

4. What can tourists do on a rainy day? ___b___

5. Can you visit a castle? ___c___

6. Where can you get a good view of the city? ___a___

a. You can go to the top of the Empire State Building.
b. They can go shopping or go to a Broadway show.
c. No, you can't. There are no real castles in New York.
d. Yes, you can. You can walk around Greenwich Village.
e. Well, you can go to an art museum or a history museum.
f. Yes, you can. You can take a walking tour, too.

About you **B** **Pair work** Ask the questions again, and give answers about your city.

A Can you visit a historic neighborhood in Tokyo?

B Let me think. . . . Well, you can visit the Yanaka neighborhood.

❌ **Common errors**

Don't use *to* after *can*.

You **can go** shopping.
(NOT ~~You can to go shopping.~~)

3 Speaking naturally *Can* and *can't*

/kən/	/kən/	/kæn(t)/
What can you do here?	*You can go to the zoo.*	*You can't go on Mondays.*

A 🔊 2.51 Listen and repeat the sentences above. Notice the pronunciation of *can* and *can't*.

B 🔊 2.52 Listen and complete the sentences below with *can* or *can't*.

1. What fun things ___can___ you do in your city?
2. What ___can't___ you do?
3. You ___can___ sit at outdoor cafés at night.
4. You _____ go to a show every night.
5. You ___can___ spend a day at the beach.
6. You _____ see live music at a club.
7. You ___can___ take a ferry to an island.
8. You ___can___ go up a tower.

About you **C** **Pair work** Are the sentences above true about your town or city? What else can and can't you do?

1 Building vocabulary and grammar

A 🔊 2.53 Listen and repeat. Check (✓) the countries you know in English. Add more.

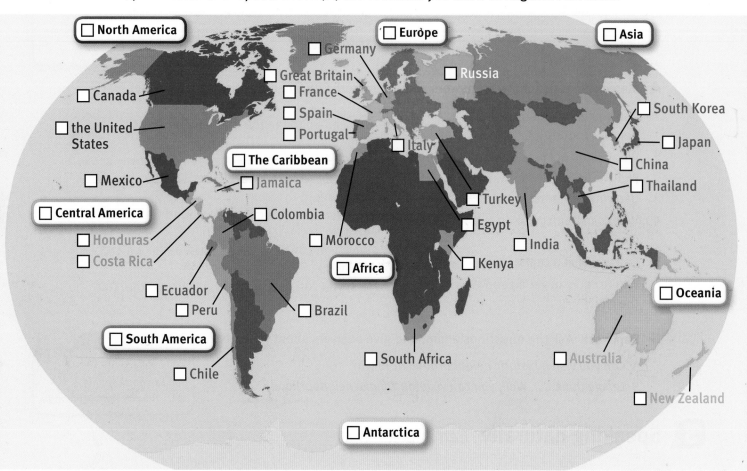

☐ North America
☐ Europe
☐ Asia
☐ Germany
☐ Russia
☐ Great Britain
☐ France
☐ Canada
☐ Spain
☐ South Korea
☐ the United States
☐ Portugal
☐ Japan
☐ Italy
☐ China
☐ The Caribbean
☐ Thailand
☐ Mexico
☐ Jamaica
☐ Turkey
☐ Central America
☐ Colombia
☐ Egypt
☐ Honduras
☐ India
☐ Costa Rica
☐ Morocco
☐ Kenya
☐ Africa
☐ Ecuador
☐ Oceania
☐ Peru
☐ Brazil
☐ South America
☐ South Africa
☐ Australia
☐ Chile
☐ New Zealand
☐ Antarctica

Word sort **B** Where do people speak these languages? Complete the chart. Then compare with a partner.

Arabic	Chinese	English	French	German	Hindi	Italian
Egypt	China	US	France	Germany	India	Italy
Japanese	**Korean**	**Portuguese**	**Russian**	**Spanish**	**Turkish**	**Thai**
Japan	South Korea	Brazil	Russia	Spain	Turkey	Thailand

Figure it out **C** Read what Claudia says about languages. Then complete the sentences.

Vocabulary notebook p. 94

> I'm from Brazil. My first language is Portuguese, but I can speak a little English, too. I can't speak Spanish, but I can understand it.

1. Claudia ___can___ speak Portuguese and English.
2. She ___can___ understand Spanish, but she ___can't___ speak it.

Claudia

2 Grammar *Can* and *can't* for ability 🔊 3.01

Extra practice p. 147

> **Use *can* to talk about things you do well. Use *can't* for things you don't do well, or don't do.**
> I **can** speak Chinese.   What languages **can** you speak?   **Can** you speak Spanish?
> I **can't** speak Spanish.   I **can** speak English and Chinese.   Yes, I **can**. / No, I **can't**.

About you Write questions using *can*. Then ask and answer the questions with a partner.

1. How many / languages / you / speak? *How many* _____
2. you / read / the news / in English? *Can you read* _____
3. What languages / you / understand / but not speak? _____
4. you / understand / movies / in English? _____
5. you / sing / a song / in English? _____
6. Who / speak / English / in your family? _____
7. you / speak / any / other / languages? _____

3 Listening and speaking International dishes

A Look at the foods below. Do you ever eat these types of food? Tell the class.

B 🔊 3.02 Listen to Richard make restaurant plans with a friend. Check (✓) the types of food he likes.

☐ Brazilian   ☑ Chinese   ☐ Indian   ☑ Italian

☑ Japanese   ☐ Mexican   ☐ Thai   ☐ Turkish

C 🔊 3.02 Listen again. Which restaurant do Richard and his friend choose? Why?

About you **D** **Pair work** Ask and answer questions about international foods. Take notes on your partner's answers. Tell the class about your partner.

Puedes cocinar
• Can you cook? What international dishes can you make? *Yes, I can. I can cook Italian food and Chinese food.*
• What are your favorite international dishes? *My favorite dishes pasta.*
• What types of food don't you like? *I don't like food is Indian food.*
• Can you find good international restaurants in your city?

"Ravi can cook very well. He can make Italian and French dishes."

1 Conversation strategy Explaining words

A How often do you order these things in a café: ice cream, soda, cake?

B 🔊 **3.03** Listen. What do Yuki and Stan order?

Server	Are you ready to order?
Yuki	Yes. Can I have a large diet soda?
Server	A large diet soda?
Yuki	Yes, please.
Stan	Um, can I have coffee ice cream with chocolate sprinkles?
Server	Sure. OK.
Yuki	What are sprinkles?
Stan	They're a kind of candy. You can put them on things like ice cream and cake. They're kind of like sugar.
Yuki	Oh, I know. You can get them in Japan, too.

C **Notice** how Stan uses *a kind of* and *kind of like*. He's explaining a new word to Yuki. Find examples in the conversation.

> *"What are sprinkles?"*
> *"They're a kind of candy."*

D 🔊 **3.04** Look at the photos. Complete the first sentence about each item with a word from the box. There is one extra word. Then listen and write the country each item comes from.

kimbap

a crêpe

gazpacho

lassi

bread	drink	dessert	snack	soup

1. Kimbap is a kind of __snack__ .   It's like Japanese sushi.   Kimbap is from __Korea__ .
2. A crêpe is a kind of __dessert__ .   It's kind of like a pancake.   They eat crêpes in __France__ .
3. Gazpacho is a kind of __soup__ .   It's kind of like tomato juice. It's from __Spain__ .
4. Lassi is a kind of __drink__ .   It's kind of like a milkshake.   Lassi is from __India__ .

E **Pair work** Take turns asking a partner to explain the words above.

> *"What's kimbap?"*   *"It's a kind of . . . "*

2 Strategy plus *Like*

You can use *like* to give examples.

> **In conversation**
>
> *Like* is one of the top 15 words.
> It has other meanings:
> I **like** Brazilian food.
> What's Thai food **like**? Spicy?
> Sprinkles are **like** sugar.

You can put sprinkles on things like ice cream and cake.

About you Imagine a tourist is asking these questions about your country. Complete the answers. Then practice with a partner.

1. A What are good souvenirs to buy?
   B Let's see. You can buy things like _alpaca sweater, t-shirt, key chains and ceramic_.

2. A Do you ever see people in traditional clothes? What are they like?
   B Well, sometimes people wear things like _skirts, poncho, ojotas_.

3. A Can you buy any traditional musical instruments?
   B Yeah, you can buy things like _harp, quena_.

4. A Where are good places to visit?
   B Well, you can visit places like _Machu picchu citadel, Kenko, Pisac ruins, Paracas reserve, lake titicaca, Huara National Park_.

3 Listening and strategies What language is it from?

A 🔊 **3.05** Listen and complete the chart. Then match the items and the photos.

Foreign word	What is it?	What language is it from?	Where is it popular?
1. *hamburger*	It's a kind of _sandwich_.	_Germany, German_	_USA_
2. *tortilla*	It's kind of like _bread_.	_Hispano America_	_Mexico_ and _central America_
3. *baklava*	It's a kind of _dessert_.	_Turkey_	_Turkey_ and _Greece_
4. *balalaika*	It's a kind of _musical instruments_	_Russia_	_Russia_

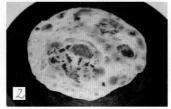

About you **B** **Pair work** Imagine you are a visitor to your country. Role-play conversations. Ask your partner to explain three words (e.g., food, clothes, an instrument).

A *What's* guacamole?
B *It's a kind of snack.*

((⋅ Sounds right p. 138

1 Reading

A What do you know about these popular tourist destinations? What can you see or do there? Make a class list.

- Bogotá
- Rio de Janeiro
- Moscow
- Beijing

B Look at the website. How many of your ideas are mentioned?

Reading tip

Before you read something, think, "What do I know about this?" and "What can I learn?"

---

http://www.travelguide...

The Travel Guide

Where can you go for a great city break? Paris? London? New York? Of course! But there are many more amazing cities to see! Click **More** to find out about these exciting destinations.

BOGOTÁ, Colombia

Bogotá is a city of contrasts. Walk around La Candelaria, a historic neighborhood with narrow streets, old churches, and modern skyscrapers! Or go to the Chapinero neighborhood, with its beautiful park, great cafés, and shops. Don't miss the Gold Museum and its beautiful jewelry exhibits. More

MOSCOW, Russia

The Kremlin Palace and the Cathedral of Saint Basil in Red Square are just some of the

historic sites you can see in Russia's capital. There are also tourist attractions *under* the city! The Moscow Metro (the subway) is full of art, statues, and crystal chandeliers. More

RIO DE JANEIRO, Brazil

Rio is famous for its beaches, mountains, and natural beauty. Walk through Tijuca National Park, or take the cable car to the top of Sugar Loaf Mountain for amazing views of the city. Or you can join the locals and head for the beach. More

BEIJING, China

In Beijing, you can experience the old and the new. Take a tour of the Forbidden City with its 600-year-old palaces. Then visit the modern Olympic "bird's nest" stadium [Beijing National Stadium]. End the day with a traditional foot massage. More

C Look at the website again. Find these things and answer the questions.
Then discuss with a partner.

- a historic neighborhood. What are the streets like?
- two cities with palaces. Where are these palaces?
- a place to get a great view. How do you get to the top?
- a city you want to visit. What do you like about this city?

 Talk about it Do you want to take a trip?

Group work What ideas do you and your classmates have about travel?

Can you agree on . . .

▶ three countries you all want to go to?
▶ three tourist attractions you want to see?
▶ three types of food you all want to try?
▶ two languages you need when you travel abroad?
▶ three really good souvenirs to buy?
▶ the three best places to visit in your country?

A Well, I want to go to Egypt.
B Yeah. You can see the Pyramids.
C Yes, it looks interesting, and I can speak Arabic.

Writing An online travel guide

A Read the extract below from a travel guide website. Notice how commas separate the different
items in a list. Can you find similar lists on the website on page 92?

Bangkok, Thailand is famous for
its palaces, temples, and
beautiful river. Visit the beautiful
Grand Palace. Walk around the
historic temples, the quiet
gardens, and the museum. Then
you can take a boat trip on the
river and enjoy the sunset.

> 🖉 **Help note**
>
> **Commas in lists**
> *Bangkok is famous for
> its **palaces, temples,
> and beautiful river.***

B Write about a place you know for the Travel Guide on page 92. Use the Travel Guide
and the extract about Bangkok to help you.

C **Pair work** Read your classmates' paragraphs. Which ones are the most interesting?

About
you **D** **Pair work** Find words in the Travel Guide with the meanings below. Then take turns using the
words in sentences about your city.

1. different things _____
2. tall buildings _____
3. the main city in a country _____
4. people who live in a place _____
5. go to _the Chapinero neighborhood._
6. "You can't do it – it's _____ ."

Free talk p. 134

Learning tip *Grouping vocabulary*

You can sort new vocabulary into groups. You can group nationalities by their endings and countries by their regions.

1 Choose 15 or more nationalities you want to learn. Write them in a chart like this. Group the nationalities by their endings.

-ese	-ian / -an / -n
Vietnamese	Colombian
Chinese	Brazilian
Portuguese.	Moroccan

-ish	Other
Spanish	Greek
British	
Polish	

2 Make a chart like this for different countries.

Africa	Asia	Europe
Morocco	Thailand	France
Egypt	South Korea	Italy

North America	Central America	South America
Mexico	Panama	Peru
Canada	Costa Rica	Ecuador

On your own

Find a world map. Label it in English.
How many countries do you know?

Some countries and nationalities	
Argentina	Argentine
Brazil	Brazilian
Canada	Canadian
Chile	Chilean
China	Chinese
Colombia	Colombian
Costa Rica	Costa Rican
Ecuador	Ecuadorian
Egypt	Egyptian
France	French
Germany	German
Great Britain	British
Greece	Greek
Iraq	Iraqi
Israel	Israeli
Italy	Italian
Jamaica	Jamaican
Japan	Japanese
Mexico	Mexican
Morocco	Moroccan
Panama	Panamanian
Peru	Peruvian
Poland	Polish
Portugal	Portuguese
Russia	Russian
Saudi Arabia	Saudi
South Korea	South Korean
Spain	Spanish
Thailand	Thai
Turkey	Turkish
United Arab Emirates	Emirati
Venezuela	Venezuelan
Vietnam	Vietnamese

✓ Can Do! Now I can . . .

✓ I can . . .   ? I need to review how to . . .

- ☐ give sightseeing information.
- ☐ say what languages I can speak.
- ☐ talk about countries and nationalities.
- ☐ explain words and give examples.

- ☐ understand people making restaurant plans.
- ☐ understand explanations of foreign words.
- ☐ read a travel website.
- ☐ write a paragraph for a travel website.

1 Questions and follow-up questions!

A Complete the questions with verbs. Then match the questions and answers. Practice with a partner.

1. What ___are___ you __wearing__ today? (wear) __d__
2. What colors ___you___ the teacher __wearing__ today? (wear) ____
3. What __happening__ in your neighborhood this week? (happen) __l__
4. What can you _____ in your neighborhood after midnight? (do) Can you _____ dancing? (go) ____
5. What do you want _____ tonight? (do) ____
6. What kinds of restaurants do you like _____ to? (go) ____
7. What languages can you _____ ? (speak) ____
8. What do you have _____ next weekend? (do) ____
9. What time do you have _____ tomorrow? (get up) ____
10. What _____ your friends _____ today? (do) ____
11. How often do you like _____ your family? (see) ____
12. What _____ you _____ about right now? (think) ____

a. There's a rock concert.
b. I want to stay home.
c. Every weekend.
d. Jeans and a T-shirt.
e. Food. I'm hungry.
f. Blue and gray.
g. English and a little Spanish.
h. They're all working.
i. I need to clean the house.
j. Well, I like Thai and Italian food.
k. No, you can't, but you can see a movie.
l. Early. I have to be at work before 8:00.

B Pair work Choose five questions and start conversations. Ask follow-up questions. How many follow-up questions can you ask for each topic?

A *What do you want to do tonight?*
B *I want to see a movie.*
A *Good idea! Do you know what movies are out?*
B *No, but we can look online.*

2 Play a word game.

Complete the chart. Write a word for each category beginning with each letter. You have two minutes! Then compare with a partner. Who has a word in every space?

Category	B	G	R	S	T
a sport or type of exercise	basketball				
a country		Greece			
a nationality			Russian		
an item of clothing or jewelry				a suit	
a color					turquoise

A *What sport begins with "B"? I have "basketball."*
B *Let's see. I have "baseball."*
A *OK, what country begins with "B"?*

3 Can you use these expressions?

Complete the conversation. Use the expressions in the box. Sometimes there's more than one correct answer. Then practice with a partner.

this	those	kind of like	Let me think	✓ That's great
that	like	a kind of	Let's see	That's too bad

Samir Grant! What are you doing here?

Grant I'm working here for the summer.

Samir Wow! _That's great_. Hey, I like your uniform. I mean, _that_ shirt is cool.

Grant Yeah, but I can't stand _this_ hat. It's so hot.

Samir _That's too bad_. Do you have to wear it?

Grant Uh-huh. So, what can I get for you?

Samir _Let me see_ .... What do you have?

Grant Um . . . we have things _like_ ice cream, frozen yogurt, smoothies. . . .

Samir What's a smoothie?

Grant It's _kind of a_ drink. It's _kind of like_ a milkshake.

Samir _Let me think_. Do I want frozen yogurt or a smoothie?

Grant Well, they're both good.

Samir Hey, do people really buy _those_ hats?

Grant Actually, they're free with the frozen yogurt.

Samir In that case, can I have a smoothie?

4 Do you have similar interests and tastes?

A Complete the sentences in the chart with your own information.

Sports	Countries and languages
I don't like to watch _____ . I want to learn (to) _____ .	I want to go to _Spain_ . I want to learn _Portuguese_ .

Colors	Clothes
I like to wear _red_ . I can't wear _light Blue_ .	I never wear _hat_ . I wear _dress_ a lot.

Seasons	Weather
I love the _summer_ . I don't like the _winter_ .	I hate to go out when it _snowing_ . I love to be outside when it _sunny_ .

B Group work Compare sentences. What do you have in common?

A I don't like to watch golf on TV.

B Me neither. I think it's boring.

C Really? I love to watch golf. But I don't like to watch baseball.

Busy lives

✓ **Can Do!** In this unit, you learn how to . . .

Lesson A
- Talk about last night using simple past regular verbs

Lesson B
- Describe the past week using simple past irregular verbs
- Ask simple past *yes-no* questions

Lesson C
- Respond to news with *Good for you*, etc.
- Say *You did?* to show surprise or interest

Lesson D
- Read about a blogger's week
- Write a blog about your week, using *after, before, when,* and *then*

Before you begin . . .

What do you do during the week? Are you busy? Do you do these things? What else do you do?

- practice a musical instrument
- go grocery shopping and run errands
- work late
- cook dinner every night

97

WE ASKED PEOPLE . . .

What did you do last night?

I tried to study for a math exam while my roommate practiced her flute. – Mari

Well, my wife rented a movie, so we watched that. But I didn't like it much. – Peter

Let me think. I stayed home, played a video game with some friends, and listened to music. That's it. – Josh

I chatted online with my friend Jay. He's living in Italy. – Stephen

I didn't want to go out, so I invited a couple of friends over, and we cooked dinner. – Melissa

I just worked late and then cleaned the house. You know – the usual. – Rachel

1 Getting started

A What do you do on a typical weeknight at home? Tell the class.

B 🔊 3.06 Listen and read. Which of the people above had fun last night?

Figure it out **C** Find the verbs the people use to talk about last night and complete the sentences. Then circle other verbs the people use to talk about the past.

1. Peter and his wife _____ a movie. Peter _____ like it.
2. Melissa and her friends _____ dinner. She _____ want to go out.
3. Rachel _____ late. She _____ watch a movie.

2 Grammar Simple past statements – regular verbs ◀)) 3.07

Extra practice p. 148

Simple past regular verbs are verb + -ed. The negative form is *didn't* + verb.

I	**played**	a video game.	I	**didn't play**	chess.
You	**studied**	math.	You	**didn't study**	English.
He	**watched**	a movie.	He	**didn't watch**	TV.
She	**wanted**	to stay home.	She	**didn't want**	to go out.
We	**cooked**	Italian food.	We	**didn't cook**	Chinese food.
They	**chatted**	online.	They	**didn't chat**	very long.

didn't = did not

Simple past endings

watch	▶	watched
invite	▶	invited
play	▶	played
study	▶	studied
chat	▶	chatted

In conversation

People use the simple present and simple past more often than any other verb form.

A Complete the sentences about last night with the simple past form of the verbs.

1. I __played__ (play) a video game.
2. I _didn't want_ (not / want) to work.
3. My best friend _called_ (call) me. We _chatted_ (chat) for a while.
4. It _rained_ (rain), so I _didn't want_ (not / want) to go out.
5. My friend and I _practiced_ (practice) guitar together.
6. I _tried_ (try) to study, but some friends _called_ (call) and they _invited_ (invite) me to a party.
7. Some friends and I _cooked_ (cook) dinner together.
8. I _watched_ (watch) a movie, but I _didn't like_ (not / like) it much.

About you **B** Pair work Make the sentences above true for you.

A I didn't play a video game last night. How about you?
B Me neither. I watched TV.

Common errors

Don't use a simple past form after *didn't*.

I **didn't clean** the house.
(NOT I ~~didn't cleaned~~ the house.)

3 Speaking naturally -ed endings

/t/ *I work**ed** on Saturday.*   /d/ *We play**ed** a game.*   /ɪd/ *I chatt**ed** online.*

A ◀)) 3.08 Listen and repeat the sentences above. Notice the -ed endings of the verbs.

B ◀)) 3.09 Listen and repeat the verbs and sentences below. Which verbs end in /t/ or /d/? Which verbs have an extra syllable and end in /ɪd/? Check (✓) the correct column.

			/t/ or /d/	/ɪd/
1.	talked	I talked to some friends from college.	✓	
2.	visited	Then I visited a classmate.		✓
3.	invited	She invited me over.		✓
4.	stayed	I stayed a couple of hours.	✓	
5.	watched	We watched a movie together.	✓	
6.	enjoyed	I really enjoyed my evening.	✓	

About you **C** Group work Tell your group one thing you did each night last week. Use the verbs from the lesson. How many things do you have in common?

"Last Sunday night I called my grandparents. How about you?"

1 Building vocabulary Irregular verbs

A 🔊 3.10 Listen and say the sentences. Check (✓) the things you did last week. Tell the class.

Last week . . .

1. ✓ I **bought** a sweater.
2. ☐ I **had** a piano lesson.
3. ✓ I **made** a lot of phone calls.
4. ✓ I **saw** three movies.
5. ☐ I **read** a couple of books.
6. ☐ I **went** to a party.
7. ☐ I **took** an exam and **got** an A.
8. ☐ I **met** someone interesting.
9. ☐ I **did** a lot of work.
   ☐ I **wrote** three reports.

B Look at the verbs in bold above. Can you figure out which verbs they are? Make a list.

bought - buy

> **i Note**
>
> Irregular simple past verbs do not end in *-ed*.
> buy ▶ bought
> *I **bought** a sweater.* (NOT I buyed a sweater.)

Word sort

C Write one thing you did at each time below. Then compare with a partner.

Yesterday	Last night	Two days ago
I bought some new jeans.	I took a shower	I called my mother.
Last week	**Last month**	**Last year**
I went to the cinema	I visited a NYC cinema	I travelled

 Vocabulary notebook p. 106

2 Building language

A ◀)) **3.11** Listen to Mei Lei take an online survey. Check (✓) her answers.

Did you have a busy week?	Yes, I did.	No, I didn't.
1. Did you have to work late every night?	✓	☐
2. Did you write any reports?	☐	☐
3. Did you get a lot of emails?	☐	☐
4. Did you have any appointments?	☐	☐
5. Did you make a lot of phone calls?	☐	☐
6. Did you go to any meetings?	☐	☐

Figure it out **B** Complete the questions about last week. Use the survey above to help you.

1. _Did_ you take a class?

2. _Did_ you go shopping?

3. Did you _cleaned_ the laundry?

4. Did you _took_ any exams?

About you **C** **Pair work** Ask and answer all the questions in Exercises 2A and 2B. How many things do you have in common?

3 Grammar Simple past *yes-no* questions ◀)) **3.12**

Extra practice p. 148

Did	you he / she we they	**go out** a lot last week? **play** tennis last weekend?	Yes, No,	I he / she we they	**did.** **didn't.**

About you **A** Unscramble the questions and write your own answers. Then ask and answer the questions with a partner. Remember your partner's answers.

1. you / early / go to bed / Did / last night / ?

   Did you go to bed early last night? Yes, I did. I went to bed at 9:00.

2. a lot of homework / you / Did / yesterday / do / ?

   Did you do a lot of homework yesterday? Yes, I did. I did a lot of homework yesterday.

3. do any errands / you / have to / Did / last weekend / ?

   Did you have to do any errands last weekend? Yes, I did. I had to visit my family in NJ.

4. have / Did / last month / a busy schedule / you / ?

   Did you have a busy schedule last month? No, I didn't.

5. last Friday / go out / Did / you and your friends / ?

   Did you and your friends go out last Friday? Yes, we did. We went to the cinema.

6. anything interesting / your best friend / do / Did / last week / ?

   Did your best friend do anything interesting last week? No, he didn't.

About you **B** **Pair work** Find a new partner. Ask and answer questions about your first partners. How much do you remember?

   A *Did Alex go to bed early last night?*

   B *No, he didn't. He went to bed after midnight.*

1 Conversation strategy Appropriate responses

A Match the questions and the expressions. Which expressions can you use when someone . . .

1. passed a test? ___d___
2. has to take a test tomorrow? ___c___
3. failed a test? ___a___
4. got an A on a test? ___b___

a. I'm sorry to hear that.
b. Congratulations!
c. Good luck.
d. Good for you.

B ◀))) **3.13** Listen. Which conversations are about good news? Which are about bad news?

1
Mark Thank goodness it's Friday.
Eve   Yeah. I'm exhausted.
Mark Me too. I had a cold all week.
Eve   You did? I'm sorry to hear that.

2
Selina So how did your
        interview at the
        hospital go?
Adam   Great! I got the job.
Selina You did? Thank
        goodness! I know you
        really wanted it.
Adam   Yeah. I start on Monday.
Selina That's great.
        Congratulations!

3
Celia Hey – happy birthday! Did you have
       a nice day?
Hugo   Yeah. Thanks. I went out for lunch
       with some friends.
Celia You did? Nice.

4
Olivia Did you take your
        driver's test yesterday?
Jake   Yeah. I failed.
Olivia Oh, you did? I'm sorry to
        hear that.
Jake   I can take it again next
        month, though.
Olivia Yeah? Well, good luck!

C Notice how the people above respond to news. They use expressions like *I'm sorry to hear that.* Find examples in the conversation.

"I had a cold all week."

"I'm sorry to hear that!"

D Write a response for each comment. Use the ideas in the box. Then practice with a partner.

1. I have a job interview this week. _____
2. I'm exhausted. I have a terrible cold. _____
3. I lost my job last week. _I'm sorry to hear that_
4. I'm 21 today! _Happy birthday!_
5. I passed my driver's test last week. _Congratulations!_
6. My sister had to go to the hospital, but she's OK. _Thank goodness!_

Good luck!
Happy birthday!
Congratulations!
I'm sorry to hear that.
Thank goodness!

"I have a job interview this week."   *"That's great. Good luck!"*

2 Strategy plus *You did?*

You can say *You did?* to show that you're interested or surprised, or just that you're listening.

I had a cold all week.

You did?

In conversation

You can also say *Did you?* to show that you're listening.

A 🔊 3.14 **Match each comment with a response. Write *a* to *e*. Then listen and check. Practice and continue the conversations with a partner.**

1. I had a nice, relaxing day at the beach last weekend. ___c___

2. I went to a new jazz club last Saturday. ___a___

3. I invited some friends over to my house last Friday night. _____

4. I stayed home on Sunday. _____

5. I took my sister to a movie for her birthday. _____

a. You did? Did you like the music?
b. Did you? Did you do chores?
c. You did? Did you go swimming?
d. Did you? Did you see anything good?
e. You did? Nice. Did you cook dinner?

About you **B** **Pair work** Tell a partner three things you did last weekend. Respond with *You did?* or *Did you?* and a follow-up question.

3 Listening and strategies *Good week? Bad week?*

A 🔊 3.15 **Listen to the conversations. What kind of week did the people have? Check (✓) the correct words.**

1. Laura: ☐ fun   ☐ busy   ☐ relaxing
2. Tyler: ☐ exhausting   ☐ bad   ☐ exciting
3. Louis: ☐ boring   ☐ terrible   ☐ interesting

B 🔊 3.15 **Listen again. Complete the sentences.**

1. Laura wrote a _____ last week. She has to present it at a _____ next week.
2. Tyler painted a picture of _____ . _____ bought it.
3. Louis's department store _____ . Now he can't _____ .

C 🔊 3.15 **Listen and respond. Choose the best response to give each person. There is one extra.**

1. Laura _____
2. Tyler _____
3. Louis _____

a. Oh, I'm sorry to hear that.
b. Did you? Well, happy birthday!
c. You did? Congratulations!
d. Really? Good for you. Well, good luck!

About you **D** **Pair work** Did you have a good week or a bad week? Tell a partner. How long can you continue your conversation?

A I had a really good week. I had to write a big essay, but I finished it.

B You did? Good for you. Did you get an A?

1 Reading

A Do you ever read blogs? Do you know people who write blogs? What topics do they write about? Tell the class.

B Read Martin's blog. What did he do last week? What problems did he have?

> **Reading tip**
>
> Writers don't always repeat the subject of two or more actions. *I invited her over, cooked . . . , and made . . .*
> (= I invited . . . , I cooked . . . , I made . . .)

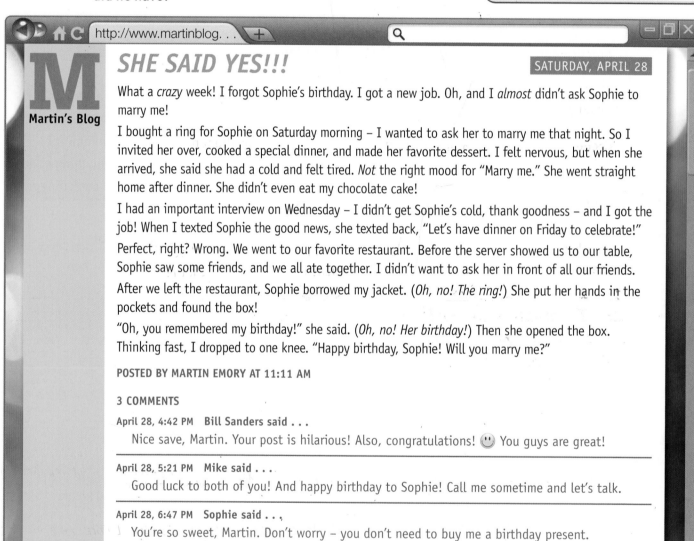

http://www.martinblog. . .

Martin's Blog

SHE SAID YES!!!

SATURDAY, APRIL 28

What a *crazy* week! I forgot Sophie's birthday. I got a new job. Oh, and I *almost* didn't ask Sophie to marry me!

I bought a ring for Sophie on Saturday morning – I wanted to ask her to marry me that night. So I invited her over, cooked a special dinner, and made her favorite dessert. I felt nervous, but when she arrived, she said she had a cold and felt tired. *Not* the right mood for "Marry me." She went straight home after dinner. She didn't even eat my chocolate cake!

I had an important interview on Wednesday – I didn't get Sophie's cold, thank goodness – and I got the job! When I texted Sophie the good news, she texted back, "Let's have dinner on Friday to celebrate!"

Perfect, right? Wrong. We went to our favorite restaurant. Before the server showed us to our table, Sophie saw some friends, and we all ate together. I didn't want to ask her in front of all our friends.

After we left the restaurant, Sophie borrowed my jacket. (*Oh, no! The ring!*) She put her hands in the pockets and found the box!

"Oh, you remembered my birthday!" she said. (*Oh, no! Her birthday!*) Then she opened the box. Thinking fast, I dropped to one knee. "Happy birthday, Sophie! Will you marry me?"

POSTED BY MARTIN EMORY AT 11:11 AM

3 COMMENTS

April 28, 4:42 PM   Bill Sanders said . . .
Nice save, Martin. Your post is hilarious! Also, congratulations! 😊 You guys are great!

April 28, 5:21 PM   Mike said . . .
Good luck to both of you! And happy birthday to Sophie! Call me sometime and let's talk.

April 28, 6:47 PM   Sophie said . . .
You're so sweet, Martin. Don't worry – you don't need to buy me a birthday present.
I love you.

C Read Martin's blog again. Are the statements true or false?
Check (✓) *True* (T) or *False* (F). Compare with a partner.

	T	F
1. Martin wanted to ask Sophie to marry him on Saturday.	☐	☐
2. Sophie went home early on Saturday because she had a cold.	☐	☐
3. Martin got Sophie's cold.	☐	☐
4. Sophie felt happy when Martin got a new job.	☐	☐
5. Martin planned a big dinner with Sophie's friends on Friday night.	☐	☐
6. Martin bought Sophie a birthday present.	☐	☐

2 Listening and speaking *Guess what I did!*

A 🔊 **3.16** Listen to three voice mail messages. What are they about?
Number the topics 1 to 3. There are two extra.

| getting in shape _3_ | work _2_ | a vacation _1_ | a new movie _____ | studying _____ |

B 🔊 **3.16** Listen again. Circle the correct words to complete the sentences.

1. Ethan ate a lot of **fast food** / **new dishes** on his trip.
2. He's learning **French** / **to cook.**
3. Alexis bought some new clothes for **her job** / **a show**.
4. She **likes to** / **doesn't like to** shop for clothes.
5. Sarah's friends think she **gets** / **doesn't get** a lot of exercise.
6. Sarah **watched TV** / **read a magazine** on her exercise bike.

About you C Group work Think of something interesting you did recently. Prepare a voice mail message to tell a classmate. Take turns telling your messages.

3 Writing A great day

A Think of a day when you had a really interesting or fun experience. What different things did you do that day? Write a list. Then number the sentences in the order you did them.

1: I ate breackfast.   5: I wacht   TV
2: I called my mother
3: I went to a school
4: I cooked dinner

B Read the blog entry below and the Help note. Underline the words in the blog that show the order of events. Then write a blog using your ideas from above. Use *before*, *after*, *when*, and *then*.

A "Thank Goodness It's Friday" Party

Last Friday, I met a friend for coffee after work. We usually go out on Fridays, but we wanted to do something different. We felt exhausted, and we wanted to relax a little! Before we left the coffee shop, we called four friends. We invited them to my apartment for a little party. Then we stopped at a supermarket and bought some sodas and three big pizzas. When our friends arrived, we just sat and talked for hours. And we ate all three pizzas! We had a really great time!

Help note

Ordering events with *before*, *after*, *when*, and *then*

I met a friend **after** / **before** class.

I called a friend **before** I went out.
Before I went out, I called a friend.

I went to bed **when** I came home.
When I came home, I went to bed.

I left work. **Then** I met a friend.

About you C Pair work Read your partner's blog. Ask questions to find out more information.

"So you sat and talked for hours. What did you talk about?"

Free talk p. 135

Sounds right p. 138

Learning tip *Making notes on verbs*

When you write down a new verb, make notes about it. Is it regular (*R*) or irregular (*Ir*)? How do you spell the different forms? How do you pronounce the endings?

	Regular?	he, she, it, -s	-ing form	Simple past
	watch (R)	watches /ɪz/	watching	watched /t/
	take (Ir)	takes /s/	taking	took

1 Make a chart like the one above. Complete it for these verbs: *study, chat, invite, do, buy,* and *meet*.

2 Here are the simple past forms of some irregular verbs you know.
Complete the chart with the verb for each simple past form.

eat	ate		felt		meant	*sel*	saw	*take*	took
buy	bought		forgot		met		sent	*go*	went
	brought		found		paid	*sleep*	slept		went out
	came		gave		put		sold		woke up
	chose	*get*	got	*run*	ran		spent		won
	cost	*have*	had	*read*	read		spoke	*wear*	wore
do	did	*VT*	knew		said		swam	*write*	wrote
drank	drank		left		sang		thought		
drive	drove	*make*	made	*sell*	sat		told		

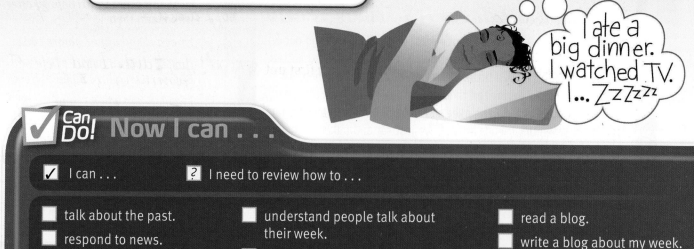

On your own

Before you go to sleep tonight, think of all the things you did today. How many things can you remember?

I ate a big dinner. I watched TV. I... ZzZzzz

✓ Can Do! Now I can . . .

✓ I can . . .   ? I need to review how to . . .

- ☐ talk about the past.
- ☐ respond to news.
- ☐ show that I'm listening.
- ☐ understand people talk about their week.
- ☐ understand voice mail messages.
- ☐ read a blog.
- ☐ write a blog about my week.

Looking back

 Can Do! In this unit, you learn how to . . .

Lesson A
- Describe past experiences
- Ask and answer questions using the past of *be*

Lesson B
- Talk about vacations
- Talk about activities with *go* and *get* expressions

Lesson C
- Show interest by answering and then asking a similar question
- Use *Anyway* to change the topic or end a conversation

Lesson D
- Read a funny magazine story
- Write a story using punctuation for conversations

1. my first friend

2 .my first home

3. my first pet

Before you begin . . .
- What do you remember about these things?
- What other "firsts" do you remember?

Getting started

A Circle the best words to complete the sentences. Are the sentences true for you?

1. I'm pleased with my grades. I'm **happy / unhappy**.
2. I'm not relaxed in exams. I'm **nervous / happy**.
3. I often make mistakes in class. It's **embarrassing / fun**.
4. I don't talk a lot. I'm **loud / quiet**.
5. I'm 18. I'm **young / old**.
6. I hate homework. It's **fun / awful**.

B 🔊 **3.17** Listen. Why was Ryan scared? Why was Melissa nervous?

The College Post

What do you remember?
We interviewed two students about some "firsts" in their lives.

Ryan Wong

The College Post: Do you remember your first teacher?

Ryan Wong: Kind of. I remember her name was Ms. Johnson and that we were all scared of her.

The College Post: Was she strict?

Ryan Wong: Yeah, she was very strict. It was awful! I was so unhappy that year – I was only five. The other kids weren't too happy either. We were all very quiet in her class.

Melissa King

The College Post: Do you remember your first job?

Melissa King: Yeah. I had a part-time job in a restaurant. I was a server. I was young – only 16. I remember that on my first day things were really busy, and I was very nervous. I made a lot of embarrassing mistakes, and my boss wasn't too pleased.

The College Post: What about the customers? Were they nice?

Melissa King: Yes, they were – I guess because I was new.

Figure it out **C** Can you complete the answers to these questions about Ryan and Melissa? Then ask and answer the questions with a partner.

1. A Was Ryan's class fun?

   B No, it wasn't. It _____ awful!

2. A _____ Ryan's teacher strict?

   B Yes, she was. She _____ *very* strict.

3. A Was Melissa's boss happy about her mistakes?

   B No, he _____ too pleased.

4. A _____ Melissa's customers nice?

   B Yes, they _____ , because Melissa _____ new.

2 Grammar Simple past of *be* ◀)) 3.18

Extra practice p. 149

I	**was** only five.	I	**wasn't** very old.	**Were** you nervous?	

I **was** only five.   I **wasn't** very old.   **Were** you nervous?
He **was** very young.   He **wasn't** happy.   Yes, I **was**. / No, I **wasn't**.
She **was** strict.   She **wasn't** very nice.   **Was** she strict?
It **was** awful.   It **wasn't** fun.   Yes, she **was**. / No, she **wasn't**.
     Was it fun?
You **were** nervous.   You **weren't** relaxed.   Yes, it **was**. / No, it **wasn't**.
We **were** quiet.   We **weren't** noisy.   **Were** they nice?
They **were** scared.   They **weren't** happy.   Yes, they **were**. / No, they **weren't**.

wasn't = was not   *weren't = were not*

A Complete these conversations with *was, wasn't, were,* or *weren't*. Practice with a partner.

1. A Do you remember your first teacher?
   B Yeah. His name ___was___ Mr. Davis.
   A ___was___ he strict with you?
   B No, he ___wasn't___. He ___was___ always very nice.

Common errors
Don't use *was* with *you, we,* or *they*.
*They **were** expensive.*
(NOT ~~They was expensive~~.)

2. A ___were___ you shy when you ___were___ little?
   B Yeah, I ___was___. I ___was___ scared to talk in class. It ___was___ awful.

3. A Tell me about your first best friend. ___Were___ you classmates?
   B No, we ___weren't___. She ___was___ in my class. We ___were___ neighbors.

4. A Did you have a favorite toy when you ___were___ a kid?
   B Yes. It ___was___ my train set. It ___was___ really cool.
   A ___was___ it a birthday present?
   B No, it ___wasn't___. I bought it with my own money.

B Pair work Ask and answer the questions. Give your own answers.

3 Speaking naturally Stress and intonation

Were you ↷nervous?   No, I ↶wasn't.   I was ↶relaxed.

A ◀)) 3.19 Listen and repeat the sentences above. Notice how the voice falls or rises on the stressed words.

B ◀)) 3.20 Listen and repeat the questions and answers below about a first English class.

1. A Was the class **eas**y?   B No, it **was**n't. It was **hard**!
2. A Were the other students **good**?   B Yes, they were all very **smart**.
3. A Were they **nice** to you?   B Yes, they **were**. They were very **friend**ly.
4. A Was your teacher **strict**?   B Yes, she **was**. But she was **nice**.

C Class activity Interview three students about their first English class. Ask the questions above.

1 Building language

A ◀)) **3.21** Listen. What did Jason do on his vacation? Practice the conversation.

Diana   Great picture! When did you get back?
Jason   Last night.
Diana   So how was your vacation?
Jason   Oh, it was wonderful.
Diana   Where did you go exactly?
Jason   We went to Hawaii.
Diana   Wow! What was the weather like?
Jason   It was hot, but not too hot.
Diana   Nice. So what did you do there?
Jason   We went to the beach every day, and I went parasailing. I didn't want to come home.
Diana   Well, I'm glad you did. . . . I have a ton of work for you!

Figure it out **B** Circle the correct words. Then ask a partner the questions.

1. A How **was** / did your last vacation?
    B It was wet. We didn't do much.

2. A Where did you **go** / went?
    B We went camping in Oregon.

3. A What **was the weather** / the weather was like?
    B It rained every day.

4. A What **did you** / you did do?
    B We played cards a lot.

2 Grammar Simple past information questions ◀)) 3.22

Extra practice p. 149

How was your vacation?	It was fun.	**Where did** you **go**?	To Hawaii.
What was the weather like?	It was hot.	**Who did** you **go** with?	A couple of friends.
Where was Jason last week?	On vacation.	**What did** you **do**?	We went to the beach.
Where were you exactly?	In Hawaii.	**Who did** Jason **go** with?	His family.
How long were you there?	A week.	**When did** they **get** back?	Last night.

About you Write questions for these answers. Then practice with a partner. Practice again, giving your own answers.

1. _How was your last vacation_ ?   It was great.
2. _____ ?   I went to Greece.
3. _____ ?   Wonderful. It was sunny every day.
4. _____ ?   My brother and sister.
5. _____ ?   We were there for a week.
6. _____ ?   We saw the Parthenon in Athens.

"How was your last vacation?"   *"It was OK. I stayed here in the city."*

(((**Sounds right p. 138**

3 Building vocabulary

A 🔊 **3.23** Listen to these memories of trips. Match the memories with the pictures.

1 "I **went hiking** with a friend in Peru, and we **got lost**. We **got** really scared when it **got** dark."

2 "I **got** a new camera from my mom for my trip to Africa."

3 "I **got sick** on our honeymoon, right after we **got married**."

4 "I **went on a trip** across Canada with a friend. It was awful. We didn't **get along**."

5 "I **went to see** a band in Miami. I met the lead singer, and **I got his autograph**."

6 "I **went snorkeling** in Thailand. It was great, but I **got a bad sunburn**."

Word sort **B** Make word webs for *get* and *go* with expressions from the sentences above. Add ideas.

go hiking

(**go**)

get lost

(**get**)

About you **C** **Pair work** Tell your partner about your best trip or vacation. What did you do?

A *Last year I went hiking with my cousin.*

B *You did? Where did you go? Was it fun?*

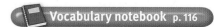 Vocabulary notebook p. 116

1 Conversation strategy Answer a question; then ask a similar one.

A What questions can you ask your friends about their weekend? Make a list.

B 🔊 3.24 Listen. How was Jessica's weekend? How was Tom's weekend?

Tom	So, how was your weekend, Jessica?
Jessica	Great! Gina and I went biking out in the country.
Tom	Oh, really?
Jessica	Yeah, it was fun, but there were lots of hills. I was exhausted by the end of the day.
Tom	Yeah, I bet.
Jessica	So . . . anyway, what did *you* do?
Tom	Oh, I had a party Saturday. It was good.
Jessica	Really? Nice.
Tom	Well, anyway, . . . I have to go. I have a meeting now. See you later.

C Notice how Jessica answers Tom's question and then asks a similar one. She shows she is interested in Tom's news, too. Find her question in the conversation.

About you **D** Answer each question. Then think of a similar question to ask. Practice your conversations with a partner.

1. A How was your weekend? Was it good?

    B *Answer:* _____

    Then ask: _____

2. A What did you do on Friday night?

    B *Answer:* _____

    Then ask: _____

3. A Did you do anything fun on Sunday?

    B *Answer:* _____

    Then ask: _____

2 Strategy plus *Anyway*

You can use *Anyway* to change the topic of a conversation.

Anyway, what did *you* do?

The party was good. Well, anyway, . . . I have to go.

You can also use *Anyway* to end a conversation.

In conversation

Anyway is one of the top 300 words.

🔊 **3.25 Listen to the conversations. Why are these people saying *anyway*? Circle *a* or *b*. Then practice with a partner.**

1. A What did you do on Saturday?

    B Not much. I slept late, went shopping. It was OK. But **anyway,** do you want to go out tonight?

    a. to change the topic
    b. to end the conversation

2. A Did you work last weekend?

    B Yeah. I had to study for an exam. I got so tired. But, **anyway,** I got a new phone last week.

    a. to change the topic
    b. to end the conversation

3. A Where were you on Sunday evening?

    B Oh, I was out. I went bowling. . . . Well, **anyway,** it's late. See you tomorrow.

    a. to change the topic
    b. to end the conversation

3 Listening and strategies Weekend fun

A 🔊 **3.26 Listen to three conversations. Which three topics do the people talk about in each conversation? Number the topics 1, 2, or 3.**

☐ biking   ☐ the movies   ☐ the beach   ☐ dancing   ☐ a party

☐ shopping   ☐ studying   ☐ hiking   ☐ a concert   ☐ a road trip

B 🔊 **3.26 Listen again. Answer the questions about each conversation.**

Conversation 1 a. What was the weather like in the mountains? _____

                                            b. What did Rex do on the weekend? _____

Conversation 2 a. What did Laura buy? _____

                                            b. What did John do? Was he home late? _____

Conversation 3 a. What didn't Emma do last weekend? _____

                                            b. Why does Joe have to go? _____

C 🔊 **3.26 Listen again. Check (✓) the conversations that end.**

☐ Conversation 1   ☐ Conversation 2   ☐ Conversation 3

About you **D Class activity Start a conversation about last weekend with a classmate. End your conversation, and then talk with another classmate. Talk to at least three people.**

1 Reading

A Do you ever read the letters people send in to magazines? What topics do people write about? Add ideas.

problems, funny stories . . .

type

Reading tip

As you read a story, stop at the end of each paragraph. Can you guess what happens next?

B Read the story from a magazine. What kind of story is it? What happened to Sarah?

Our community:
This week – funny stories from our readers

How embarrassing!
By Sarah Morgan

llena de gente

A funny thing happened to me yesterday after work. I was really hungry and I didn't feel like making dinner, so I went to a fast-food place near my office building. I got a cheeseburger, some fries, and a soda. The restaurant was really crowded, so I had to share a table. I sat down with my tray across from a young guy. I said, "Hi. Is this seat free?" He nodded and smiled, but he didn't say anything. He seemed pretty nice.

Anyway, I got out a magazine and started eating my burger. It was a really interesting article and I couldn't stop reading. But then I saw the guy take one of my fries! I couldn't believe it, but I was too embarrassed to say anything. Then he took another one, and I still didn't say anything!

desconcertada embarazada

Then I thought, "Those are my fries." So I took a handful and ate them. The guy looked at me in a funny way, but he didn't say anything. Then he did it again and ate another one of my fries! It was really strange.

Finally, a few minutes later, he got up, took his tray, and left. That's when I realized the fries were on his tray! And my fries? They were under my magazine. How embarrassing! I ran out into the street. There was the guy.

Continued on next page . . .

C Read Sarah's story again. Then match the two parts of each sentence.

1. Sarah had dinner at a fast-food place because ___h___
2. The restaurant was crowded, so ___d___
3. Before Sarah sat down at the young guy's table, ___e___
4. Sarah was surprised when the guy ate some fries because ___f___
5. Sarah didn't say anything about the fries because ___b___
6. The guy gave Sarah a funny look when ___g___
7. When the guy left the table with the fries on his tray, ___a___
8. When Sarah looked under her magazine, ___c___

a. she realized they were *his* fries.
b. she was very embarrassed.
c. she found her own fries.
d. she had to sit with someone.
e. she said, "Hi. Is this seat free?"
f. she thought they were *her* fries.
g. she started eating some fries.
h. she didn't want to cook.

2 Writing He said, she said

A Read the Help note and Sarah's story again. Notice the punctuation. Then add punctuation to the rest of her story below.

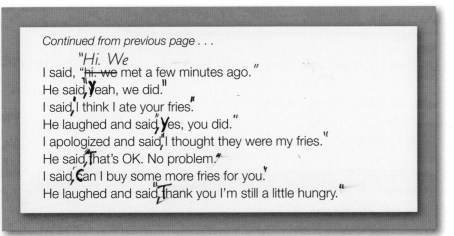

Continued from previous page . . .

"Hi. We

I said, "hi. we met a few minutes ago."
He said, "Yeah, we did."
I said, "I think I ate your fries."
He laughed and said, "Yes, you did."
I apologized and said, "I thought they were my fries."
He said, "That's OK. No problem."
I said, "Can I buy some more fries for you?"
He laughed and said, "Thank you I'm still a little hungry."

Help note

Punctuation with speech
• Use quotation marks (" ") *quotation* around the things people say.
• Use a comma (,) after **said.**
• Use a capital letter to start a quotation.
  I said, "Is this seat free?"
  He said, "Sure."

B What did they say next? Write six sentences to finish the story. Be sure to use the correct punctuation for things people say. Read your ending to the class.

3 Listening and speaking Funny stories

A 🔊 3.27 Listen to Miranda and John tell part of a story. Circle the correct information.

I did something really embarrassing about a month ago. . . .

Miranda

I said something once to a dinner guest. . . .

John

1. Miranda was **at work** / **in a store.**
2. Her friend **loves** / **hates** shopping.
3. They looked at a **dress** / **sweater.**
4. Miranda **liked** / **didn't like** the colors.

5. John was **10** / **20** years old.
6. His father's **boss** / **friend** came for dinner.
7. John and the man talked about **school** / **work.**
8. John **liked** / **didn't like** his new teacher.

B 🔊 3.28 Choose the best ending for each story. Circle *a* or *b*. Then listen and check your guesses.

1. Miranda's story
   a. Then my friend said, "Actually, I bought one last week."
   b. The clerk said, "Do you like this season's colors?"

2. John's story
   a. My teacher said, "You look tired. Were you up late last night?"
   b. My teacher said, "I hear you met my father last night."

About you **C** **Pair work** Retell one of the stories above to a partner, or tell a funny story of your own.

Free talk p. 135

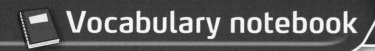

Vocabulary notebook | Past experiences

Learning tip *Time charts*

You can use a time chart to log new vocabulary. Look at the example below.

1 Complete the sentences on the time chart with the correct verbs from the box. You can use a verb more than once.

bought	had	took	didn't have	went
got	✓lived	was	didn't get along	

Time in the past	Event or experience
15 years ago	My family ___*lived*___ in Hawaii.
10 years ago	I _____ in high school.
5 years ago	I _____ my driver's license and _____ my first car.
2–4 years ago	I _____ my first trip abroad.
last year	I _____ sick and _____ in the hospital for two weeks.
last month	My brother _____ married and _____ to Fiji on his honeymoon.
last week	My friend Jo _____ a party. It _____ boring. I _____ a good time.
last weekend	I _____ hiking with a friend. It was awful – we _____ .

2 Make a time chart like the one above. Write about your past experiences.

 On your own

Make a time chart, and put it on your wall. Look at it every day.

Last week: I started a new job.
Last month : I was on vacation.

Can Do! Now I can . . .

✓ I can . . .	? I need to review how to . . .

- ☐ describe past school, work, and travel experiences.
- ☐ talk about activities with *go* and *get* expressions.
- ☐ show interest by answering then asking a question.
- ☐ change the topic or end a conversation.

- ☐ understand conversations about weekends.
- ☐ understand people telling funny stories.
- ☐ read a funny magazine story.
- ☐ write a story that includes conversations.

Fabulous food

✓ **Can Do!** In this unit, you learn how to . . .

Lesson A
- Talk about eating habits using countable and uncountable nouns, *How much,* and *How many*

Lesson B
- Talk about food
- Make offers using *Would you like . . .* and *some* or *any*

Lesson C
- Use *or something* and *or anything* in lists
- End *yes-no* questions with *or . . . ?* to be less direct

Lesson D
- Read a restaurant guide
- Write a restaurant review

1
2
3

4
5
6

Before you begin . . .

Match the pictures with the food categories. Which foods did you eat yesterday?

5 **grains:** bread, rice, and pasta
1 **dairy:** milk and cheese
2 **seafood:** fish and shellfish

6 **meat:** beef and chicken
3 **vegetables:** broccoli and carrots
4 **fruit:** bananas and a papaya

Voice-mail greeting: We're not home right now. Please leave a message.

Hi, Mom and Dad! I need some help fast! I invited some friends for dinner tonight, and I don't know what to cook.

Amy's a vegetarian, so she doesn't eat meat, fish, cheese, or eggs. I guess she just eats a lot of fruits and vegetables, and maybe rice.

Juan's on a diet. He can't eat much rice, bread, or pasta. But he eats a lot of meat, cheese, eggs, and vegetables, like carrots and cucumbers.

And David is picky – I mean, he doesn't eat many vegetables. And he's allergic to milk and shellfish. But he likes potatoes. Oh, and bananas. Please call me! Bye.

1 Getting started

A What are some foods that the people below don't eat? Make a list.

- a vegetarian   • a "picky" eater   • a person on a diet   • a person with food allergies

B 🔊 3.29 Listen. Ellen is leaving a message for her parents. What is her problem? Which plate of food does Ellen think is right for Amy? for Juan? for David?

Figure it out **C** Find the food words in Ellen's message. Are they singular or plural? Write them in the chart. Then circle *a lot of*, *much*, and *many*. Do singular or plural nouns follow the words?

Singular			Plural		
meat	rice	milk	eggs	potatoes	vegetables
fish	bread	shellfish	carrots	bananas	
cheese	pasta		cucumbers	fruits	

About you **D Pair work** Which of the foods above do you like? Which don't you like? Tell a partner.

A *I love meat. How about you?*

B *Um, I don't eat meat, but I like fish and vegetables.*

118

2 **Grammar** Countable / uncountable nouns 🔊 **3.30**

Extra practice p. 150

Countable nouns	**Uncountable nouns**
Examples: an apple, six potatoes	Examples: cheese, meat, fish
Use *a / an* or plural *-s*:	**Don't use *a / an* or plural *-s*:**
I have **an egg** for breakfast every day.	I drink **milk** every morning.
I don't eat **bananas**.	I don't eat **seafood**.
Use *how many*, *a lot of*, and *many*:	**Use *how much*, *a lot of*, and *much*:**
How many eggs do you eat a week?	**How much milk** do you drink a day?
I eat **a lot of eggs**.	I drink **a lot of milk**.
I don't eat **a lot of eggs**.	I don't drink **a lot of milk**.
I don't eat **many** (**eggs**).	I don't drink **much** (**milk**).

A Circle the correct words in these conversations. Then practice with a partner.

1. A How **much / many** fruit do you eat a day?

    B Well, I have **banana / a banana** every day for breakfast,
    and I eat **much / a lot of** fruit after dinner for dessert.

2. A How **much / many** times a week do you eat **potato / potatoes**?

    B About once a week. But I eat **rice / the rice** every day.

3. A Do you eat **many / a lot of** red meat?
    Or do you prefer **chicken / the chicken**?

    B Actually, I'm a vegetarian, so I never eat **meat / meats**.

4. A How often do you eat **seafood / the seafood**?

    B Well, I eat **much / a lot of** fish, but I'm allergic to **shellfish / a shellfish**.

5. A How **much / many** eggs do you eat a week?

    B I don't eat **much / many**. I don't really like **egg / eggs**.

6. A How often do you eat **vegetable / vegetables**?

    B I usually eat **much / a lot of** French fries. Is that a vegetable?

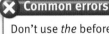

✖ Common errors

Don't use *the* before nouns to talk about food in general.

I don't like meat, but I eat eggs. (NOT ~~I don't like the meat, but I eat the eggs.~~)

About you **B** **Pair work** Ask and answer the questions. Give your own answers.

3 **Talk about it** What's your diet?

Group work Discuss the questions. Do you have similar habits?
Then tell the class one interesting thing about a person in your group.

▸ Are you a picky eater? What foods do you hate?
▸ Are you allergic to any kinds of food? What are you allergic to?
▸ Are you on a special diet? What can't you eat?
▸ How many times a day do you eat?
▸ Do you ever skip meals?
▸ In your opinion, what foods are good for you? What foods aren't?
▸ Do you have any bad eating habits? What are they?

1 Building vocabulary

A 🔊 3.31 Listen and say the words. Which foods do you like? Which don't you like? Tell the class.

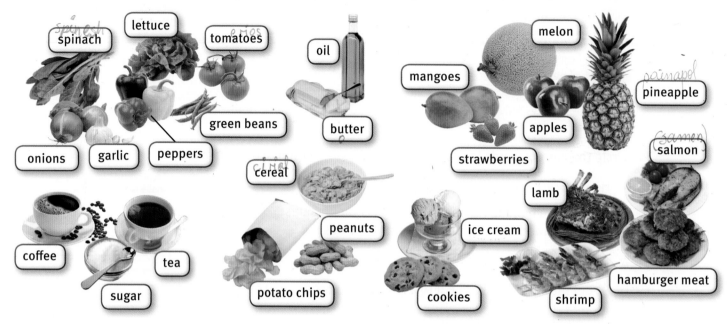

spinach · lettuce · tomatoes · oil · melon · mangoes · pineapple · apples · butter · green beans · strawberries · salmon · onions · garlic · peppers · cereal · lamb · peanuts · ice cream · coffee · tea · sugar · potato chips · cookies · shrimp · hamburger meat

Word sort

B Complete the chart with the foods above. Add ideas. Then tell a partner about your diet.

meat	seafood	vegetables	fruit	dairy	grains	drinks	snacks	other
lamb Hamburg	clams shrimp	Spinach, lettuce Tomatoes peppers green beans onions garlic	mangoes, melon pineapple apple strawberries		Su	Coffee Tea	potato chips	ice cream oil butter

" I eat a lot of lamb."   "I don't eat many clams."   "I don't eat much ice cream."

Vocabulary notebook p. 126

2 Building language

A 🔊 3.32 Listen. What do Ted and Phil have to do before dinner? Practice the conversation.

Ted I guess it's my turn to cook dinner. So what would you like?

Phil Um, I'd like some chicken. Do we have any?

Ted Um, no, we need to get some. We don't have any vegetables, either. Would you like to go out for pizza?

Phil Again? No, I think I'd like to stay home tonight.

Ted OK. Then we have to go to the grocery store.

Phil Well, I went grocery shopping last week. I think it's your turn.

Figure it out

B Circle the correct words. Then practice with a partner.

1. A What would you **like / like to** eat?
   B I'd **like / like to** some chicken.

2. A I'd like **some / any** fish.
   B We don't have **some / any**. Let's go buy **some / any**.

3 Grammar *Would like; some and any* ◄)) 3.33

Extra practice p. 150

Use *would like* **+ to +** verb
or *would like* **+** noun.
Would you **like to** go out?
    No, I**'d like to** stay home.

What **would** you **like** for dinner?
    I**'d like** some chicken.

Would you **like** some tea?
    Yes, please. / No, thanks.

I'd = I would

Use *some* in affirmative statements and *any*
in questions and negative statements.
Do we have **any** vegetables?
    Yes, we have **some** (vegetables).
    No, we don't have **any** (vegetables).

Do we have **any** chicken?
    Yes, we have **some** (chicken).
    No, we don't have **any** (chicken).

📃 **In conversation**

Any is common in questions:
    Do you have **any** *cookies?*
Some is common in questions
that are offers or requests:
    Would you like **some** *chicken?*
    Can I have **some** *chocolate?*

A Complete the conversations. Use *some, any, would . . . like,* or *'d like.*
Sometimes there are two correct answers.

1. A I'm sleepy. I'd like to go for a walk. __Would__ you ___like___ to come?

    B Sure. Let's go out for _____ coffee. I _____ to get _____ cake, too.

2. A I'm really thirsty. Do you have _____ water with you?

    B Well, I have _____ soda. Would you like _____ ?

3. A _____ you _____ a snack? I have _____ cookies and peanuts.
       Oh wait, I don't have _____ peanuts.

    B Um, I _____ some fruit. Do you have _____ ?

4. A What _____ you _____ to do after class? Do you have _____ plans?

    B Well, I need to go shopping and get _____ food.

    A Oh, I can come with you. I need to get _____ milk, too. I don't have _____ .

B **Pair work** Ask and answer the questions. Give your own answers.

    A *I'm sleepy. I'd like to go for a walk. Would you like to come?*
    B *Sure. Let's get some soda, too.*

❌ **Common errors**

Always add *to* when *I'd like*
is followed by a verb.

I'd like to go for a walk.
(NOT ~~I'd like go for a walk.~~)

---

4 Speaking naturally *Would you . . . ?*

What **would you** like?   **Would you** like a snack?   **Would you** like to have dinner?

A ◄)) 3.34 Listen and repeat the questions above. Notice the pronunciation of *Would you . . . ?*

B ◄)) 3.35 Listen and complete the questions. Then listen again and practice.

1. What would you like to _____ ?
2. Would you like to _____ ?
3. Would you like to _____ ?
4. Where would you like to _____ ?
5. What would you like to _____ ?

C **Pair work** Make dinner plans with a partner. Use the questions above.

1 Conversation strategy *or something* and *or anything*

A What kinds of food are popular for lunch? Make a list.

B 🔊 3.36 Listen. What do Carrie and Henry decide to do for lunch?

Carrie	Let's take a break for lunch.
Henry	Sure. Would you like to go out or . . . ?
Carrie	Well, I just want a sandwich or something.
Henry	OK. I don't want a big meal or anything, either. But I'd like something hot.
Carrie	Well, there's a new Spanish place near here, and they have good soup.
Henry	That sounds good.
Carrie	OK. And I can have a sandwich or a salad or something like that.
Henry	Great. So let's go there.

C **Notice** how Carrie and Henry use *or something (like that)* and *or anything*. They don't need to give a long list of things. Find examples in the conversation.

"I just want a sandwich or something."

D Complete the conversations with *or something* and *or anything*. Then practice with a partner.

1. A Do you eat a big lunch?

   B No, I usually just have a salad _____ .

2. A What do you usually have for breakfast?

   B Oh, I just have some coffee and a muffin _____ .

   A You don't have eggs _____ ?

3. A Would you like to go out for dinner _____ ?

   B Sure. But I don't want a big meal _____ . Something light maybe.

   A OK. Well, let's go somewhere with a salad bar _____ .

> **Note**
>
> Use *or something* in affirmative statements and in questions that are offers and requests.
>
> Use *or anything* in negative statements and most questions.

About you **E** **Pair work** Ask and answer the questions. Give your own answers.

2 Strategy plus *or . . . ?*

You can use *or . . . ?* at the end of *yes-no* questions to make them less direct.

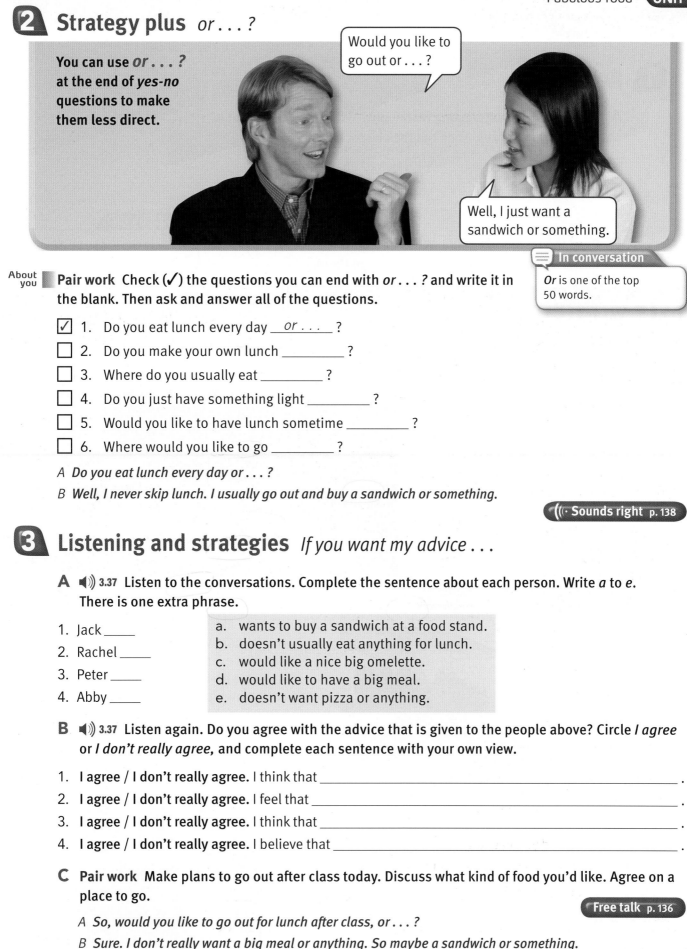

> Would you like to go out or . . . ?

> Well, I just want a sandwich or something.

In conversation

Or is one of the top 50 words.

About you **Pair work** Check (✓) the questions you can end with *or . . . ?* and write it in the blank. Then ask and answer all of the questions.

✓ 1. Do you eat lunch every day __*or . . .*__ ?

☐ 2. Do you make your own lunch _____ ?

☐ 3. Where do you usually eat _____ ?

☐ 4. Do you just have something light _____ ?

☐ 5. Would you like to have lunch sometime _____ ?

☐ 6. Where would you like to go _____ ?

A Do you eat lunch every day or . . . ?

B Well, I never skip lunch. I usually go out and buy a sandwich or something.

((· Sounds right p. 138

3 Listening and strategies *If you want my advice . . .*

A 🔊 3.37 **Listen to the conversations. Complete the sentence about each person. Write *a* to *e*. There is one extra phrase.**

1. Jack _____
2. Rachel _____
3. Peter _____
4. Abby _____

a. wants to buy a sandwich at a food stand.
b. doesn't usually eat anything for lunch.
c. would like a nice big omelette.
d. would like to have a big meal.
e. doesn't want pizza or anything.

B 🔊 3.37 **Listen again. Do you agree with the advice that is given to the people above? Circle *I agree* or *I don't really agree,* and complete each sentence with your own view.**

1. **I agree / I don't really agree.** I think that _____ .
2. **I agree / I don't really agree.** I feel that _____ .
3. **I agree / I don't really agree.** I think that _____ .
4. **I agree / I don't really agree.** I believe that _____ .

C **Pair work** Make plans to go out after class today. Discuss what kind of food you'd like. Agree on a place to go.

Free talk p. 136

A So, would you like to go out for lunch after class, or . . . ?

B Sure. I don't really want a big meal or anything. So maybe a sandwich or something.

1 Reading

A Do you know an interesting restaurant? What's special about it? Check (✓) the boxes. Then tell the class.

☐ It has a nice atmosphere. ☐ It has a beautiful view.
☐ It has live music. ☐ It has good service.
☐ It serves unusual food. ☐ other _____

B Read the restaurant guide. Which restaurant would you like to try? Tell a partner why you'd like to go there.

> **Reading tip**
> As you read, imagine each place. Ask yourself, "Would I like to eat there?"

 Restaurant Guide: Try something different!
We searched the world and found these unusual places to eat.

Chillout ice restaurant, Dubai

Would you like to visit a *really* cool restaurant? Then try this place. Everything is made of ice, from the tables and chairs to the pictures on the walls. When you order a soda, it comes in an ice glass, and your meal is served on an ice plate. Luckily, if you get too cold, you can ask for a warm blanket and some hot chocolate. Be sure to try some ice cream, too. It never melts!

Dinner in the Sky, in over 35 countries

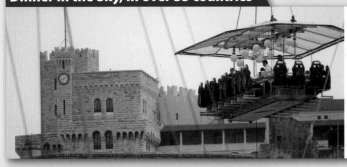

How would you like to dine 50 meters (164 feet) above your favorite view? Then hire Dinner in the Sky for a special event. You and 21 guests can enjoy dinner at a table hanging in the air! A chef, a server, and an entertainer go with you to make a perfect evening. But if you're scared of heights, we don't recommend it!

The Hajime Robot Restaurant, Bangkok

Here's something *really* different – a restaurant with robots. Choose your food from a touchscreen computer menu, and a few minutes later, a smiling robot brings it to you. You can also barbecue food at your table or order other delicious Asian dishes from the menu. Try a green tea smoothie and then sit back and enjoy the entertainment – every hour the robots dance to music! It's a fun and lively atmosphere, and the service is excellent!

C Read the article again, and answer these questions. Explain your answers to a partner.

1. What can you do if you feel cold at the Chillout ice restaurant?
2. What dish does the writer recommend there?
3. How many people can dine in the sky at one time?
4. Who goes up with the guests at Dinner in the Sky?
5. What can you order at the Hajime Robot Restaurant?
6. Why do you think people try restaurants like these?

2 Listening and writing Do you recommend it?

A 🔊 3.38 Listen to Olivia talk about a restaurant she went to last week. What do you find out about it? Circle the correct words.

1. The restaurant was **Italian / Spanish**.
2. They serve great **seafood / pasta**.
3. Olivia had **a rice dish / a seafood salad**.
4. It's good for **meat eaters / vegetarians**.
5. The service was **fast / slow**.
6. The atmosphere was **fun / relaxed**.
7. It was **expensive / inexpensive**.
8. Olivia **recommends it / doesn't recommend it**.

B Read the review and the Help note. Underline the adjectives that describe the Healthy Bites restaurant.

> **RESTAURANT REVIEW: Healthy Bites**
>
> Last week I had dinner at a small neighborhood restaurant called Healthy Bites. It serves healthy fast food, and it is famous for its hamburgers. The food is excellent. The hamburgers come with delicious toppings like spicy cabbage with onions and a lot of garlic. The service was excellent – fast but friendly. I highly recommend it.

Help note

Useful expressions

Was it . . .	good?	bad?
The restaurant was	good.	terrible.
The service was	excellent.	slow.
The servers were	friendly.	unfriendly.
The meal was	delicious.	awful.
The food was	tasty.	tasteless.
The potatoes were	hot.	cold.

About you **C** Write a review of a restaurant you know. Talk about the atmosphere, the food, the service, and the price.

D Read your classmates' reviews. Which restaurant would you like to try?

3 Talk about it What are your favorite places to eat?

Group work Discuss the questions. Agree on a place you'd like to go to together.

- How often do you go out to eat?
- When you eat out, do you go to restaurants? cafés? fast-food places? food stands?
- Do you have a favorite place to eat? Where is it? Why do you like it?
- Where can you get good, cheap food?
- Where can you hang out with friends?
- Which restaurant in your city would you like to try?
- Which restaurant don't you recommend? Why not?

4 What's the right expression?

Complete the conversation with these expressions. (Use *anyway* twice.) Then practice with a partner.

or something	Good for you	anyway	Congratulations	You did
✓ or anything	good luck	I know	thank goodness	I'm sorry to hear that

Bryan How was your weekend? Did you go away _or anything_ ?

Julia No, but I went to a karaoke club.

Bryan Really? _____ ? So how was it?

Julia Great! I sang in a contest and won $50.

Bryan _____ ! I didn't know you were a singer.

Julia Well, I practiced every day for a month.

Bryan _____ !

Julia And _____ I practiced! Ten of my friends were there. So, _____ , did you do anything special?

Bryan Not really. I had to study for an exam on Saturday and Sunday. I studied all weekend and then got sick.

Julia _____ . You need to take care of yourself.

Bryan Yeah. _____ . . . . Well, _____ , I have to go. I want to study my notes. But after the exam, let's meet for coffee _____ .

Julia OK. So _____ with your exam.

5 Show some interest!

A Complete each sentence with a simple past verb. Then add time expressions to five sentences to make them true for you.

1. I _went_ on an interesting trip.   *I went on an interesting trip last month.*
2. I _____ some new clothes.
3. I _____ someone famous.
4. I _____ an international phone call.
5. I _____ a party at my house.
6. I _____ some Italian food.
7. I _____ on the beach.
8. I _____ English with a tourist.
9. I _____ some money.
10. I _____ lost in the city.

B **Pair work** Take turns telling a partner your sentences. Respond with *You did?* and ask questions.

A *I went on an interesting trip last month.*

B *You did? Where did you go? . . .*

UNIT
7 **Find out about your classmates.**

1 **Class activity** Find classmates who answer *yes* to the questions. Write their names in the chart. If someone answers *yes*, ask a follow-up question to find out more information.

Find someone who . . .	Name	More information
is taking music lessons.	Joani	Yes, I'm
is in a band.	Angelly	nao, I not
is working two jobs.	Argentina	no, I not
is looking for a new job.	Miyabi	no, I not
is eating out a lot these days.	Armando	no, I not
isn't getting enough sleep.	Jenifer	yes, I'm
is playing on a sports team.	Yesenia	yes, I'm
isn't getting enough exercise.	Israel	no, I not
is shopping for a new laptop or cell phone.	Nanami	no, I not
is writing a blog.		

A *Are you taking music lessons?*
B *Yes, I am. I'm taking piano lessons.*
A *That's great. How are they going?*
B *Great. I'm learning a lot.*

2 **Class activity** Tell the class one interesting thing you found out about a classmate.

UNIT
8 **Think fast!**

Group work Think of an idea for each item below. You have two minutes! Then compare ideas with your group. Does anyone have the same answers?

Think of . . .
- a gift you have to get for someone _____shoes_____
- something you need to buy _____sandals_____
- a store you need to go to _____mayous_____
- something you don't want to do, but you have to do _____Laund_____
- a sport you want to try _____pilatis_____
- a sport you don't want to try _____Karate_____
- something you like to wear to class _____pink_____
- something you need to do after class _____cook_____
- something you have to wear to a wedding _____dress_____ formal - long dress gown
- a TV show you like to watch _____Sex and the city_____
- someone you need to call _____my boyfriend_____

UNIT
9 **Where in the world?**

1 **Pair work** Where in the world can you do these things? Use the photos to help you.

Where can you . . .

1. see an amazing palace?
2. see a historic neighborhood?
3. take a cable car?

4. swim at a beautiful beach?
5. hear traditional music?
6. take a boat trip on a river?

Istanbul, Turkey

Rio de Janeiro, Brazil

Mexico City, Mexico

Merida, Venezuela

Paris, France

Tokyo, Japan

2 **Pair work** Choose a country you know about. Brainstorm ideas about all the interesting things you can do there. Explain any new words to your partner.

A *OK, let's make a list for Australia.*

B *Well, you can see some amazing animals, like koalas.*

A *What's a koala?*

B *Oh, it's kind of like a little bear. They're gray and white.*

UNIT **10** **Yesterday**

1 Look at Mario's apartment. What did he do yesterday? Study the picture for two minutes. Then close your book and make a list. How much can you remember?

2 **Pair work** Compare your lists. Did you do any of the same things as Mario? Tell your partner.

A *Did Mario do the laundry yesterday?*
B *Yes, he did. I have that on my list.* **OR** *I don't know. I don't have that on my list.*
A *Yeah, I did my laundry and my roommate's laundry yesterday.*
B *You did? Good for you.*

UNIT **11** **Guess where I went on vacation.**

1 Choose a beautiful or exciting city or country. Imagine you went there on vacation. Think of answers to these questions. Write notes in the chart.

How did you get there? Did you take a train or bus? Did you fly? Did you drive?	I flew
How long did the trip take?	The trip took 23 hours.
What time of year was it?	It was summer.
4 What was the weather like?	It was hot
5 What did you do there?	I visited my family, went to see...no, and went sho...
6 What did you wear?	I wore dresses, shorts, and T-shirts.
7 What kind of food did you eat?	I ate rice, noodles, and meat
8 What souvenirs did you buy?	I bought clothes and traditional crafts.
9 What language do they speak there?	They spoke Filipino

2 **Pair work** Ask questions like the ones above (but not "Where did you go?") to guess where each person went on vacation. How many questions do you need to guess the city or country?

A *How did you get there? Did you fly?*
B *No, I took the bus.*
A *OK. So how long did the trip take? Was it a couple of hours?*

UNIT **12** **Give it a try.**

1 Complete the chart. Try and write the same ideas as other classmates. Write your ideas in two minutes.

Think of something . . .	
a picky eater doesn't eat.	
tasty for breakfast.	
you have in your refrigerator that most people don't have.	
you drink a lot of.	
you would like to try for dinner.	
you don't have much of in your kitchen.	
a vegetarian would like to eat.	

2 **Group work** Compare your ideas. Score one point each time you have the same answer as a classmate. Who has the most points?

A *Well, picky eaters don't eat much seafood or fish or anything.*

B *That's true. I wrote vegetables.*

C *I wrote seafood. So Miki and I both get a point because we have the same answer.*

3 **Group work** Find out your classmates' tastes. Ask about the things you wrote in the chart above.

A *Do you eat a lot of seafood or . . . ?*

C *No. We never have any in the house!*

Sounds right

UNIT **7**   ◀)) **3.45** Listen and repeat the words. Notice the underlined sounds. Are the sounds like the sound in _four_ or the sound in _word_? Circle the correct word.

1. le<u>ar</u>n (f<u>our</u> / w<u>or</u>d)
2. m<u>or</u>ning (f<u>our</u> / w<u>or</u>d)
3. p<u>er</u>fect (f<u>our</u> / w<u>or</u>d)
4. sp<u>or</u>t (f<u>our</u> / w<u>or</u>d)
5. w<u>ar</u>m (f<u>our</u> / w<u>or</u>d)
6. w<u>or</u>k (f<u>our</u> / w<u>or</u>d)

UNIT **8**   ◀)) **3.46** Listen and repeat the words. Notice the underlined sounds. Check (✓) the sounds that are like the sound in _hat_.

☐ 1. b<u>a</u>ckp<u>a</u>ck ☐ 4. neckl<u>a</u>ce ☐ 7. briefc<u>a</u>se ☐ 10. sungl<u>a</u>sses
☐ 2. m<u>a</u>ll ☐ 5. br<u>a</u>celet ☐ 8. s<u>a</u>le ☐ 11. j<u>a</u>cket
☐ 3. bl<u>a</u>ck ☐ 6. p<u>a</u>nts ☐ 9. c<u>a</u>p ☐ 12. w<u>a</u>tch

UNIT **9**   ◀)) **3.47** Listen and repeat the words. Notice the underlined sounds. Are the sounds like the sound in _she_ or the sound in _child_? Write _sh_ or _ch_.

1. Chile _ch_
2. Fren<u>ch</u> ____
3. Portugue<u>s</u>e ____
4. Spani<u>sh</u> ____
5. <u>Ch</u>inese ____
6. informa<u>ti</u>on ____
7. ques<u>ti</u>on ____
8. stat<u>u</u>e ____
9. <u>ch</u>ocolate ____
10. natu<u>r</u>al ____
11. Ru<u>ss</u>ian ____
12. <u>s</u>ugar ____
13. delic<u>i</u>ous ____
14. o<u>c</u>ean ____
15. <u>sh</u>ow ____
16. Turki<u>sh</u> ____

UNIT **10**   ◀)) **3.48** Listen and repeat the words. Notice the underlined sounds. Are the sounds like the sounds in _looked_, _bought_, _spoke_, or _left_? Write the words from the box in the correct columns below.

br<u>ou</u>ght	c<u>oo</u>ked	m<u>e</u>t	r<u>ea</u>d	s<u>aw</u>	t<u>o</u>ld
ch<u>o</u>se	dr<u>o</u>ve	p<u>u</u>t	s<u>ai</u>d	th<u>ou</u>ght	t<u>oo</u>k

looked	bought	spoke	left
cooked	brought	chose	met
put	Thought	drove	read
took	Saw	Told	said

UNIT **11**   ◀)) **3.49** Listen and repeat the words. Notice the underlined sounds. Which sound in each group is different? Circle the odd one out.

1. h<u>ar</u>d p<u>ar</u>t sc<u>ar</u>ed sm<u>ar</u>t
2. aut<u>o</u>graph rel<u>a</u>xed nerv<u>ou</u>s par<u>a</u>sailing
3. f<u>ir</u>st n<u>er</u>vous sn<u>or</u>keling w<u>or</u>ry
4. b<u>a</u>ck ex<u>a</u>ctly h<u>a</u>ppy vac<u>a</u>tion

UNIT **12**   ◀)) **3.50** Listen and repeat the words. Which syllable in each word is stronger than the other syllable(s)? Underline the stressed syllables.

1. <u>but</u>ter
2. pasta
3. carrot
4. pepper
5. cucumber
6. potato
7. pizza
8. sugar
9. melon
10. tomato
11. onion
12. water

UNIT 7 Lesson A Present continuous statements

A Complete these text messages using the verbs in parentheses.

FROM: Ava Williams   4:00 p.m.

Hey, Olivia! I hope you _not working_ (not / work). The weather is so beautiful! I _having_ (have) coffee with Lily at an outdoor café. We_'re chatting_ (chat) about work and things. And she _is checking_ (check) the Internet for a good movie. Are you free tonight? XXOO, Ava

---

FROM: Brandon Brown   5:00 p.m.

Hey, John. Eric and I_'m relaxing_ (relax) here at the beach. Eric _is swimming_ (swim), and I_'m sending_ (send) text messages! But we_'re getting_ (get) hungry now. There's a great new restaurant near here. Let's meet for dinner. –Brandon

---

FROM: Olivia Martinez   4:05 p.m.

Ava, I'm not at work. I'm home with my parents, but we_'re working_ (work) very hard! My mother _cleaning_ (clean) the car, and my father and I_'m doing_ (do) the laundry. I_'m not having_ (not / have) much fun! But I'm free around 5:00 p.m. Call me! –Olivia

---

FROM: John Harris   5:30 p.m.

Brandon, I'm sorry, but I_'m staying_ (stay) home this weekend. I_'m studying_ (study) for exams. Also, I_'m writing_ (write) an essay for my English class. So I_'m not go out_ (not / go out) all weekend. Let's do something after my exams, OK? –John

---

About you **B Pair work** Imagine it's Saturday evening. Write a text message to tell your partner what you're doing. Then answer your partner's message.

> **✕ Common errors**
>
> Check the spelling of verb + *-ing*.
>
> *having* (NOT ~~haveing~~)
> *shopping* (NOT ~~shoping~~)

UNIT 7 Lesson B Present continuous questions

A Complete these phone conversations with present continuous *yes-no* and information questions. Use the words in parentheses. Compare with a partner.

1. A Hi, it's Jeremy. How are things?

    B Pretty good. So what's up? _Where are you calling_ from? (where / you / call)

    A From work. I have a new job.

    B Really? _where were you working_? (where / you / work)

    A At Angelo's Pizza. You know, with Mike.

    B Oh, right. _Is he working_ tonight? (he / work)

    A No, he's not. He only works during the day.

    B OK. _Are you taking_ a break right now? (you / take)

    A Yeah. I'm having pizza! I love this job! . . .

2. A Hi, it's me, Lauren. _Am I calling_ at a good time? (I / call)

    B Sure. I'm just watching TV.

    A Oh. _what are you watching_? (what / you / watch)

    B A rock concert on Channel 10.

    A Wow. _who are singing_? (who / sing) She has a great voice!

    B I'm not sure. But, yeah, she's amazing.

About you **B Pair work** Practice the conversations. Then practice again with your own information.

UNIT **8**

Lesson A *Like to, want to, need to, have to*

A Use the words given to complete the questions.

1. (you / like / wear) <u>Do you like to wear</u> _____ a different outfit every day?
2. (your family / like / go) _____ shopping together?
3. (you and your friends / want / go) _____ to the mall this weekend?
4. (you and your friends / like / wear) _____ the same colors?
5. (your parents / need / buy) _____ something new for your home? I mean, (what / they / have to / get) _____ ?
6. (you / like / look around) _____ electronics stores?
7. (Where / your best friend / like / buy) _____ his or her clothes?

About you **B** **Pair work** Ask and answer the questions. Give your own information.

UNIT **8**

Lesson B *How much . . . ?; this, these; that, those; saying prices*

A Look at the pictures. Complete the conversations with words from the box.
You need to use some words more than once. Sometimes there is more than one answer.

| it | they | this | that | these | those | is | are |

1. Clerk Can I help you?

   Sophia Yes. This _____ a great jacket. How much is _____ ?

   Clerk Um, . . . _____ jacket is $199, I believe.

   Sophia And what about _____ pants? How much _____ they?

   Clerk I think _____ 're $119.

   Sophia Wow. _____ 're expensive! Um . . . I have to think about it. But thanks anyway.

2. Clerk Do you need some help?

   Austin Yeah. How much _____ those sweatshirts? There's no price tag.

   Clerk _____ ? They're $29.99. They're on sale.

   Austin And what about _____ sweatpants? How much are _____ ?

   Clerk Uh, these _____ $19.75. They're on sale, too.

   Austin OK. I want to try on a blue sweatshirt and blue sweatpants.

About you **B** **Pair work** Practice the conversations with a partner. Can you think of a different ending for each conversation?

UNIT
9 **Lesson A** *Can* and *can't* for possibility

A Complete these questions and answers with *can* or *can't* and one of the verbs in the box. You can use some verbs more than once. Then practice with a partner.

do   eat   buy   go   ride   swim   take   walk

1. A What ___can___ you ___do___ for exercise in your neighborhood?
   B You ___can___ ___ride___ a bike in the park, and you ___can___ ___swim___ at the pool.

2. A What international restaurants ___can___ you ___go___ to?
   B You ___can___ ___eat___ at Chinese, Korean, and Thai restaurants.

3. A ___Can___ you ___buy___ the latest fashions in your neighborhood? (Barrio)
   B Yes, you ___can___. There's a great store near my house.

4. A ___Can___ people ___walk___ around your neighborhood late at night? *neiborhut*
   B Well, you ___can___ ___do___ a walk in the park. It's not a good idea.

5. A ___Can___ people ___take___ a ferry to work in your city?
   B No, they ___Can't___. But they ___can___ ___go___ to work by subway or bus.

> **Common errors**
>
> Use a simple verb after *can* and *can't*.
>
> *I can* **take** *the bus.*
> (NOT *I can* ~~taking~~ *the bus.*)

About you **B** **Pair work** Ask and answer the questions. Give your own answers.

UNIT
9 **Lesson B** *Can* and *can't* for ability

A Unscramble the questions. Then compare with a partner.

1. What sports / you / play well / can _What sports can you play well_?
2. you / play / Can / a musical instrument _Can you play a musical instrument_?
3. ride / a motorbike / you / Can _Can you ride a motorbike_ ?
4. drive / can / in your family / Who _Who can drive in your family_?
5. you / Can / name / all the countries in South America _Can you name all countries in South America_?
6. music / read / you / Can _Can you read music_ ?
7. international / you / cook / any / Can / foods _Can you cook any international food_?
8. speak / or understand / What languages / you / can _What languages can you speak or understand_ ?

About you **B** **Pair work** Ask and answer the questions. Give your own answers.

Extra practice

10 Lesson A Simple past statements: regular verbs

A Complete these statements with a past form of the verbs in parentheses.

1. It _rained_ (rain) yesterday, so I _didn't walk_ (not / walk) home from work.
2. I _didn't work_ (not / work) late last night because I _wanted_ (want) to go to the gym.
3. My parents _didn't want_ (not / want) to cook last night, so we _ordered_ (order) food from a restaurant.
4. I _tried_ (try) to call my best friend last night, but she _didn't answer_ (not / answer) her phone.
5. A classmate _texted_ (text) me last night, and then we _chatted_ (chat) online.
6. I _didn't clean_ (not / clean) the house on Saturday. I just _relaxed_ (relax).
7. I _needed_ (need) to go shopping for some new clothes on Saturday, but I _didn't have_ (not / have) time.
8. The neighbors _invited_ (invite) us over for dinner on Sunday. We really _loved_ (love) the food.

About you **B** **Pair work** Choose five of the sentences above and make them true for you. Tell your partner.

10 Lesson B Simple past *yes-no* questions

A Complete these questions and answers with *did, didn't,* and the verb in parentheses. Then practice with a partner.

1. A _Did_ you _went_ (go) shopping last weekend?
   B Yes, I _did_. I _bought_ (buy) a new jacket.

2. A _Did_ you _get up_ (get up) early today?
   B No, I _didn't_. I _slept_ (sleep) late this morning.

3. A _Did_ you _have_ (have) a big breakfast?
   B No, I _didn't_. I just _____ (have) coffee.

4. A _Did_ you _spend_ (spend) time on the computer last night?
   B Yes. I _did_ (do) some work. I _____ (write) a report.

5. A _Did_ your best friend _go out_ (go out) with you last weekend?
   B Yes, she _did_. We _____ (see) a movie together.

6. A I didn't come to class last week. _Did_ the teacher _give_ (give) us homework?
   B No, he _didn't_. But he _____ (give) us a test.

> **✕ Common errors**
>
> In questions, don't use a simple past form after *did.*
>
> **Did** you **go** shopping? (NOT ~~Did you went~~ shopping?)

About you **B** **Pair work** Ask and answer the questions. Give your own answers.

Lesson A Simple past of *be*

A Unscramble the questions. Then complete the answers with *was, wasn't, were,* or *weren't*.
Practice with a partner.

When you were little . . .

1. A strict / your / Were / parents *Were your parents strict?*

   B No, they _____weren't_____ very strict with me. They _____were_____ pretty relaxed about things.

2. A school / Was / elementary / your / big _____Was your elementary school big_____?

   B No, it _____wasn't_____. It _____was_____ a small school with 50 children.

3. A in / class / your / Were / friends / your _____Were your friends in your class_____?

   B Yes, they _____were_____. We _____were_____ all in the same class.

4. A a good student / Were / you _____Were you a good student_____?

   B Well, I _____was_____ OK. I always did my homework.

5. A nice / your / Was / teacher / first _____Was your first teacher nice_____?

   B My first teacher _____was_____ nice, but some teachers _____were_____ very strict.

6. A you / on / Were / a sports team _____Were you on a sports team_____?

   B No, I _____wasn't_____ on a sports team, but I _____was_____ a good swimmer.

About
you **B** **Pair work** Ask and answer the questions. Give your own information.

Lesson B Simple past information questions

A Complete the questions in the conversation. Use a question word and a verb in the simple past.
Then practice the conversation with a partner.

Jim   I see you're back in the office. *How was* _____ your vacation?

Liz   It was great. Really exciting.

Jim   So _____where did you_____ go?

Liz   I went to Brazil. To the Amazon.

Jim   Wow! _____How long were you_____ there?

Liz   I was there for over a week. It was wonderful.

Jim   It sounds great. So _____what did you_____ do exactly?

Liz   Well, I went on a boat trip — a nature tour. There were about 40 other people on
      the boat. And there was a guide. It was amazing.

Jim   Nice. So _____what was the guide_____ like?

Liz   He was smart and very interesting. I learned a lot.

Jim   And _____how was_____ the weather?

Liz   Oh, it was hot and humid. And I mean, *very* hot!

Jim   Really? So _____when did they get_____ back?

Liz   Actually, I got back four days ago. I always rest for a couple of days after a vacation!

About
you **B** **Pair work** Think about a trip you took. Start a conversation like the one above.

UNIT
12 **Lesson A** Countable / uncountable nouns

A Complete the questions with *much*, *many*, or *a lot of*. Sometimes there is more than one answer. Complete the answers with *a* or *an*. Write (–) if you don't need *a* or *an*.

1. A How ___*much*___ fish do you eat? Do you eat a lot?

   B Actually, I don't like _____ – _____ fish. I'm kind of picky.

2. A Do you eat _____ vegetables?

   B Actually, I eat _____ raw carrot every day for my mid-morning snack.

3. A How _____ fruit do you eat?

   B Well, I love _____ apples. I usually have _____ apple after dinner.

4. A Do you eat _____ red meat?

   B No, I don't. I don't like _____ red meat.

5. A How _____ cereal do you eat for breakfast?

   B I don't eat cereal. I usually have _____ egg with toast.

6. A How _____ times a week do you go out for dinner?

   B Once or twice a week. I'm a big fan of _____ Italian restaurants.

> ✖ **Common errors**
>
> With uncountable nouns, don't use *a / an* or add -*s*.
>
> *I just had some milk.*
> (NOT *I just had a milk / some milks.*)

About
you **B** **Pair work** Ask and answer the questions. Give your own answers.

UNIT
12 **Lesson B** *Would like; some and any*

A Unscramble the questions. Then complete the conversations with *some* or *any*. Compare with a partner.

1. A Would / some / you / coffee / like *Would you like some coffee?*

   B Sure, but we don't have ___*any*___ milk. I can get ___*some*___.

2. A you / like / Would / go out / to / for lunch _____?

   B Actually, I just ordered a big pizza. Would you like _____?

   A I'd love _____. I'm starving. I didn't have _____ breakfast.

3. A some / like / cookies / Would / you _____?

   B No, thanks. I don't want _____ right now. But can I have _____ later?

4. A tonight / to / Where / eat / would / like / you _____?

   B Well, there are _____ good seafood restaurants around here. I'd really like _____ fish.

5. A like / do / to / would / What / you / for your birthday _____?

   B I'd like to invite _____ friends over for dinner. But I don't want _____ gifts!

About
you **B** **Pair work** Ask and answer the questions. Give your own answers.

SECOND EDITION

TOUCHSTONE

WORKBOOK 1B

MICHAEL MCCARTHY

JEANNE MCCARTEN

HELEN SANDIFORD

CAMBRIDGE
UNIVERSITY PRESS

Contents

1 What's the weather like?

Vocabulary | **A** Write two sentences about each picture.

1. _It's hot._
   It's sunny.

2. _____

3. _____

4. _____
   _____

5. _____
   _____

6. _____
   _____

B Answer the questions. Write true answers.

1. How many seasons do you have in your city? What are they? _My city have their_
   seasons. Autumn, winter, Spring and summer.

2. What's your favorite season? Why? _My favorite season is summer,_
   because I like go to the beach.

3. What kind of weather do you like? Cold weather? Hot weather? _I like Hot weather._
   _____

4. What's the weather like today? Is it warm? _Today is rain_
   _____

5. What's the weather usually like at this time of year? _____
   _____

6. Does it ever snow in your city? If yes, when? _____
   _____

2 I'm waiting for a friend.

Grammar | **Complete the conversation. Use the present continuous.**

Erin Hi, Ken. It's Erin. Where are you?

Ken Oh, hi, Erin. I'm at the beach. I _'m spending_ (spend)

the day with Tom. It's beautiful here today! It's, uh . . .

Erin Nice. . . . I'm so happy you _are having_ (have) fun.

Ken Yeah. We _are relaxing_ (relax).

We _aren't doing_ (not do) anything

special – I mean, I _'m reading_ (read)

a book, and Tom _is swimming_ (swim).

How about you? Are you at work?

Erin No. I'm _not working_ (not work) today.

Ken Oh, right. So, where – oops! Uh, I'm sorry.

I'm _eating_ (eat) ice cream. I'm starving.

Erin Yeah, me too. I'm _eating_ (eat) a cookie.

Ken Really? So, where are you? I mean, are you at home?

Erin No, I'm at Pierre's Café. I _am waiting_ (wait)

for a friend. He's very late.

Ken Oh, really? Who?

Erin You!

3 About you

Grammar and vocabulary | **Are these sentences true or false for you right now? Write _T_ (true) or _F_ (false). Then correct the false sentences.**

1. __F__ I'm eating dinner right now.
    I'm not eating dinner right now. I'm doing my homework.

2. __F__ I'm using a computer.
    I'm not using my computer. I'm studying.

3. _____ My family is watching TV.
    Yes, they're.

4. __F__ My friends are working.
    No, they're not working now. They're going to the shopping.

5. _____ It's snowing.
    No, it isn't snowing. It's hot no.

6. _____ My best friend is skiing.
    My best friend isn't skiing, he's at the beach.

1 All about sports

Vocabulary | **A** Write the names of the sports or kinds of exercise under the pictures.

1. _volleyball_

2. _bowling_

3. _Weigh training_

4. _shunbning_

5. _Biking_

6. _basketball_

7. _Karate_

8. _Aerobic_

9. _futball_

B Complete the chart with the words in part A.

People play . . .	People do . . .	People go . . .
volleyball		

C Answer the questions. Write true answers.

1. What sports do you play? How often? _I play volleyball on Wednesdays and_
   basketball on the weekends.

2. What sports do your friends play? _____
   _____

3. Do you ever go biking? _____
   _____

4. What sports do people in your country like? _____
   _____

2 **What are you doing?**

Grammar | **Complete the conversations with present continuous questions.**

1. Joe   Hey, Luis! <u>_What are you doing_</u>   (What / you / do) ?

   Are you at home?

   Luis   No, I'm at the park. I'm playing tennis.

   Joe   Really? _____ (you / play)

   with Janet?

   Luis   No, I'm playing with John today.

   Joe   Oh. So, _____ (you / have / fun) ?

   Luis   No, I'm not. You know, it's raining here, and it's cold.

   Joe   That's too bad. _____ (you / play)

   right now? In the rain?

   Luis   Yes, we are. And it's my turn to serve. Hold on a minute. . . .

   Joe   So, um, _____ (you / win) ?

   Luis   Uh, no. I'm not playing very well today.

   Joe   Is it because you're talking on your

   cell phone?

2. Janet   Hi, Kelly. _____ (How / you / do) ?

   Kelly   Hi. Great. How are you? _____ (you / work)

   this summer?

   Janet   Yes, I'm working at a gym. I'm teaching there. It's fun.

   Kelly   Really? _____ (What / you / teach) ?

   Janet   Aerobics.

   Kelly   Cool. So, _____ (you / do) other things?

   I mean, _____ (you / swim), too?

   Janet   Yeah. There's a pool at the gym. So, _____

   (you / do) anything special this summer?

   Kelly   Well, no. I'm living in my sister's apartment. She's in

   San Francisco this summer.

   Janet   Really? _____ (What / she / do)

   there?

   Kelly   She's working in a restaurant.

   Janet   _____ (she / meet) a lot of

   new people?

   Kelly   Oh, yes. She's having a good time.

1 Keep the conversation going!

Conversation
strategies Complete the conversation with the follow-up questions in the box.

Where are you working?	✓ What are you doing?
Are you practicing your languages?	So, why are you studying Spanish and Portuguese?
What classes are you taking?	Are you enjoying your classes?

Alex   Hey, Kate. How's it going?

Kate   Good. How are things with you?

Alex   Great. But I'm really busy this summer.

Kate   Really? *What are you doing?* _____

Alex   Well, I'm taking a couple of classes, and I'm working.

Kate   Wow! You're working and studying? _____

Alex   I'm taking Spanish and Portuguese.

Kate   That's interesting. _____

Alex   Yeah, I really am. I'm learning a lot!

Kate   That's great. _____

Alex   Well, I'm thinking about a trip to South America.

Kate   That's exciting!

Alex   Yeah, and that's why I'm working two jobs, you know.

Kate   Right. _____

Alex   Well, I'm working at a Peruvian restaurant from 11:00 to 5:00, and I'm working at a Brazilian music club at night.

Kate   Really? Wow! _____

Alex   Yes, I am! I'm speaking Spanish all day and Portuguese all night.

Kate   That's really cool! But when do you sleep?

Alex   That's a problem. Sometimes I sleep in class.

Kate   Oh, right. That *is* a problem.

2 Asking follow-up questions

Conversation strategies | Complete two follow-up questions for each comment.

1. "I don't play sports, but I often go running with a friend."

Really? Where *do you go running* ?
How often _____ ?

2. "My parents are on vacation this month."

That's nice. Where _____ ?
Are they _____ ?

3. "My grandparents are visiting this week."

Really? Where _____ ?
How often _____ ?

4. "I'm working nights this summer."

Really? Where _____ ?
What time _____ ?

3 Oh, that's good.

Conversation strategies | Read these people's comments about their summer activities. Complete the responses. Then ask follow-up questions.

1. I'm really enjoying my vacation this summer.

Oh, that's ___*good*___ .
*What are you doing* ?

2. I'm not doing anything exciting. I'm just reading a lot.

That's _____ .
_____ ?

3. I'm not enjoying this summer at all. I'm working ten hours a day.

Really? That's _____ .
_____ ?

4. I'm just relaxing, and I'm watching a lot of TV.

Hey, that's _____ .
_____ ?

5. I'm exercising a lot at the gym this summer.

That's _____ .
_____ ?

6. What vacation? I'm painting my house right now.

Really? That's _____ .
_____ ?

1 An advice column

Reading | **A** Which sports and exercises do you do? Check (✓) the boxes.

- ☐ aerobics
- ☐ basketball
- ☐ biking
- ☐ running
- ☐ skiing
- ☐ soccer
- ☐ volleyball
- ☐ weight training

B Read the advice column. Match the problems with the Sports Professional's advice.

FITNESS TALK

Do you have a question about exercise? Write to Steven, the Sports Professional, for help and good advice.

1. John: I never exercise. I drive to work, and I sit all day. I hate sports, and I don't like the gym. I know it's a good idea to exercise, but how do I start? _____

2. Amy: I'm really busy this year. I'm going to school, and I'm working part-time at night. I like exercise, but I don't have a lot of time. Help! _____

3. Bill: I do weight training at the gym every day. I usually love exercise, but these days, it's boring. I think I need a break. What do you think?

a. The Sports Professional: Slowly add exercise to your weekly routine. Walk or ride a bike to work – don't drive. Use the stairs, not the elevator. Clean the house, or do the laundry. Just do something – and start today!

b. The Sports Professional: You're right. You need a break. Try exergaming for a change. There are a lot of different types of activities, and each one helps your body in a different way. Don't stop your weight training, and remember, running is always good for you, too.

c. The Sports Professional: Yes, I know the problem, but try and make time. Experts say we need 30 minutes of exercise five times a week. So, do aerobics for 15 minutes in the morning. Go to school. Then go running for 15 minutes in the evening after work.

C Read the advice column again. Then answer the questions.

1. Is John getting enough exercise these days? _____

2. Does John like sports? _____

3. Amy is busy this year. What is she doing? _____

4. What is Amy's problem? _____

5. How often does Bill go to the gym? _____

6. What does Bill do at the gym? _____

2 Write your own advice.

Writing **A** Look again at the advice column on page 56. Find two imperatives the Sports Professional uses in each piece of advice.

Try exergaming for a change.

B Make imperatives for advice. Match the verbs with the words and expressions.

(Don't)	be buy do drive exercise watch	aerobics in the morning at least five times a week shy some good running shoes to work TV all the time	*Don't be shy.* *Buy some good running shoes.*

C Read the problems. Reply to each person. Give two pieces of advice using imperatives. Use the ideas above or your own ideas.

1. **Joe:** I watch sports on TV all the time. I'm watching the Olympics this month. It's great, but I don't do any sports. What sports are fun?
   The Sports Professional: *Try a lot of different sports. I like volleyball, tennis, and swimming. Also,* _____

2. **Anita:** This fall, we're playing soccer at school. I'm not enjoying it very much, especially when it's cold! Also, I'm not very good. Help!
   The Sports Professional: _____

3. **David:** I like exercise, but I'm lazy! I usually exercise for two or three weeks, but then I need a break. Do you have any advice?
   The Sports Professional: _____

Unit 7 Progress chart

What can you do? Mark the boxes. ☑ = I can . . .　　　　? = I need to review how to . . .	To review, go back to these pages in the Student's Book.
☐ make present continuous statements. ☐ ask present continuous questions.	66 and 67 68 and 69
☐ name at least 6 words to talk about the weather. ☐ name at least 10 sports and kinds of exercise.	65, 66, and 67 67 and 68
☐ ask follow-up questions to keep the conversation going. ☐ react to things people say with *That's* . . . expressions.	70 and 71 71
☐ use imperatives to give instructions and advice.	73

Grammar

Vocabulary

Conversation strategies

Writing

1 **Do a crossword puzzle.**

Vocabulary | **A** Complete the crossword puzzle. Write the names of the clothes.

Down

1.    3.

5.    7.

8.    10.

11.

Crossword puzzle:
- 1 (down): S
- 2 (across): h i g h h e e l s
- 3 (down): T I
- 4 (across): J e a n s
- 9 (across): T H O R I T
- 11 (across): S N K E E R S
- 12 (across): D R E S S

Across

2.    4.    6.

9.    11.    12.

B Now find the five highlighted letters in the puzzle. What do they spell?

___ ___ ___ ___ _s_

58

2 I want to spend some money!

Grammar | **Complete the conversations with the correct form of the verbs.**

1. Mia   Let's go shopping. I _need to buy_ (need / buy) some new clothes.

   Rick   OK. Where do you _____ (want / go) ?

   Mia   To the mall. I _____ (need / get)
   some new jeans. And I _____ (have / get)
   a couple of new suits for work.

   Rick   Listen. You go. I think I _____ (want / stay)
   home. I _____ (not need / buy) anything,
   and I _____ (want / check) my email.

   Mia   OK!

2. Will   I have a date with Megan tonight. She _____ (want / go)
   to an expensive restaurant.

   Ana   Really? Do you have any good clothes?
   Those old jeans are terrible. And you know Megan –
   she _____ (like / wear) designer clothes.

   Will   I know, but I _____ (like / wear) my jeans!
   And I _____ (not want / go) to a
   restaurant anyway. I _____ (want / go) to a movie.

   Ana   Oh, there's the phone. Hello? . . . Will, it's Megan. She's sick.

   Will   Oh, no! Well, now I _____ (not have / change) my clothes!

3 About you

Grammar and vocabulary | **Unscramble the questions. Then write true answers.**

1. A to the movies / do / like / What / to / wear / you ? _What do you like to wear to the movies?_
   B _____

2. A nice / have / When / do / to / clothes / you / wear ? _____
   B _____

3. A you / Do / a / have / uniform / to / wear ? _____
   B _____

4. A buy / Do / like / you / to / online / things ? _____
   B _____

5. A clothes / do / What / want / you / buy / to ? _____
   B _____

6. A do / go / like / Where / you / to / shopping ? _____
   B _____

1 Accessories

Vocabulary | Write the words under the pictures using *a* or *some*.

1. <u> *some jeans* </u>
2. <u> *a dress* </u>
3. _____
4. _____

5. _____
6. _____
7. _____
8. _____

9. _____
10. _____
11. _____
12. _____

13. _____
14. _____
15. _____
16. _____

2 Colors

Vocabulary | Complete the color words in the box. Then answer the questions, and complete the chart. Write three colors to answer each question, if possible.

r_e_d   y_____   w   b_____   k   p_____   e   w_____   e
o_____   e   b____e   g_____n   b_____n   g____y

What colors . . .			
do you like to wear?	*blue*		
are you wearing right now?			
do you never wear?			
are in your home?			
are your favorites?			
are popular right now?			
are in your country's flag?			

③ How much is this?

Grammar **A** Complete the conversations. Use *this*, *that*, *these*, or *those*.

1. Lena Um, excuse me. How much is ___*that*___ dress?

    Clerk The red dress? It's $325.

    Lena Oh. And how about _____ shoes?

    Clerk They're $149.

    Lena Oh, really. And what about _____ T-shirts?
    Are they expensive, too?

    Clerk They're $49.

    Lena Oh, well. Thanks anyway.

2. Tito Excuse me.

    Seller Yes?

    Tito How much are _____ umbrellas?

    Seller They're $19.99.

    Tito $19.99? Really?

    Seller Oh, wait. Sorry. _____ umbrella is $4.99.
    _____ umbrellas over here are $19.99.

    Tito OK, so I want _____ umbrella, please.

B Look at the pictures. Write questions and answers.

1.

$99.99

A *How much are those boots?*

B _____

2.

$38

A _____

B _____

3.

$40

A _____

B _____

4.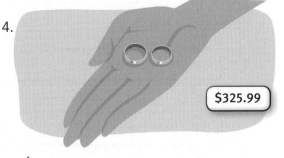

$325.99

A _____

B _____

Can I help you?

1 Um, uh, oh!

Conversation strategies Complete the chart with the "conversation sounds" and expressions in the box.

✓ I know.	Let's see.	Really?	Uh,	Um,	Yeah.
Let me think.	Oh.	Right.	Uh-huh.	Well,	

You want to show you agree.	You are surprised.	You need time to think.
I know.		

2 About you

Conversation strategies Answer the questions with true information. Start each answer with a "time to think" expression.

1. What's your favorite color?

   Let me think. . . . I guess it's green.
   _____

2. What's your favorite thing to wear?

   _____
   _____

3. How often do you shop online?

   _____
   _____

4. How much do jeans cost these days?

   _____
   _____

5. How many birthday presents do you have to buy this month?

   _____
   _____

6. Does your family like to shop for clothes together?

   _____
   _____

3 Are you listening?

Conversation
strategies | **Complete the conversation with the correct expressions.**

Roberto	Mom, I have to get some things for college.
Mother	_____*Uh-huh.*_____ What do you need to get?
	(Uh-huh. / Let me think.)
Roberto	_____ . . . I need to get a new computer and . . .
	(Um, let's see. / Really!)
Mother	_____ They're expensive.
	(Let me think. / Oh, really?)
Roberto	I know. But I have to go online a lot for my classes.
Mother	Well, OK. And what else do you want?
Roberto	_____ I want to get a new cell phone and . . .
	(Uh-huh. / Uh, well . . .)
Mother	_____ I'm surprised. I mean,
	(Oh, / Um,)
	you usually don't call, so . . .
Roberto	Well, I text sometimes. Anyway, _____ Oh, yes, and
	(let's see. / uh-huh.)
	I have to get some new sneakers.
Mother	_____ You really need new sneakers. Those sneakers are really old.
	(Let me think. / Uh-huh.)
Roberto	And what else? _____ What else do I need to get?
	(Oh, really? / Uh, let's see.)
Mother	Well, there's one more thing you need to get . . .
Roberto	What's that?
Mother	A job! You need to pay for these things!

1 Online shopping

Reading | **A** **Read the article. Who likes to shop online? Who doesn't like to shop online? Check (✓) the correct boxes.**

	Likes to shop online	Doesn't like to shop online
Sarah	☐	☐
Matt	☐	☐
Kevin	☐	☐
Susana	☐	☐

Do you like to shop online?

These days *everything* is for sale online – from movie tickets and food, to cars and houses. More and more people download music, movies, magazines, and books. It's easy and convenient. But not *everyone* likes to shop online.

Sarah Cho

"I never shop on the Internet because I like to pay cash. I don't have a credit card, and I don't want to get one. Also, I don't like to spend a lot of time online. I guess I'm not a big fan of shopping."

Matt Carson

"I work long hours – from 9:00 in the morning to 9:00 or 10:00 at night. A lot of stores close at 9:00. But the Internet never closes. I mean, I often shop at 1:00 in the morning. And the prices online are usually really cheap."

Kevin Parker

"There isn't a shopping center near my house. I have to drive an hour to the mall. Online shopping is very convenient. I buy movies, books, clothes, and food online. I never need to go out to a store."

Susana Rivera

"I like to shop with friends. We get up early and go to the mall together. We have a great time. We have lunch and look at the clothes together. When you shop online, you don't spend time with friends. You're alone."

B **Read the article again. Then write *Sarah*, *Matt*, *Kevin*, or *Susana* next to the statements.**

1. "I don't like to shop online or in stores!" _____*Sarah*_____

2. "I like to shop online because I never have to leave my home." _____

3. "I like to shop online because the prices aren't expensive." _____

4. "I don't like to shop online because I like to go to the mall with friends." _____

5. "I like to shop online because I don't have time during the day." _____

6. "I don't like to shop online because I don't like to go on the Internet." _____

2 What do you think?

A Why do people like to shop online? Why do people hate to shop online? Check (✓) the correct box.

I like to shop online . . .	I hate to shop online . . .	Reasons
☐	☐	because I always buy things I don't need.
☐	☐	because it's easy to compare prices.
☐	☐	because it's convenient.
☐	☐	because you don't always have to pay sales tax.
☐	☐	because I often get "spam" emails from shopping websites.

B Answer these questions. Try to write more than *Yes* or *No*.

1. Do you live near a mall or shopping center? _____

2. Do you have time to shop during the week? _____

3. Do you like to go online? _____

4. Do you use a credit card? _____

C Write a short paragraph. Use your ideas from part B, and give reasons. Start like this:
I like to shop online because . . . **or** *I don't like to shop online because . . .*

_____

_____

_____

_____

Unit 8 Progress chart

What can you do? Mark the boxes. ✓ = I can . . . ? = I need to review how to . . .	To review, go back to these pages in the Student's Book.
Grammar ☐ use *like to*, *want to*, *need to*, and *have to* with other verbs. ☐ ask questions with *How much . . . ?* ☐ use *this*, *these*, *that*, and *those*.	76 and 77 78 and 79 79
Vocabulary ☐ name at least 12 kinds of clothes. ☐ name at least 12 accessories. ☐ name at least 8 color words.	75, 76, and 77 78 and 79 78
Conversation strategies ☐ use "time to think" expressions like *Um, . . .* and *Let's see . . . .* ☐ use *Uh-huh* and *Oh,* to show that I agree or I'm surprised.	80 81
Writing ☐ use *because* to give reasons.	83

A wide world

Lesson A / Sightseeing

1 Take a tour!

Vocabulary | **A** Complete these suggestions for tourists.

1. In South Korea, visit _an island_ .

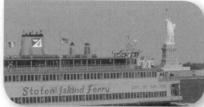

2. In New York, take pictures from a _____ .

3. In Germany, visit an old _____ .

4. See a _____ of a famous writer in Paris.

5. In Rio de Janeiro, spend a day at the _____ .

6. In Egypt, walk around the _____ .

7. In London, see a famous _____ .

8. Go up a _____ and get a good view of Tokyo.

9. Take a _____ of the city in Sydney.

Grammar and vocabulary | **B** Can you do any of the things in part A in your city or town? Write true sentences.

1. _In my area, you can visit an island._   **or**   _In my area, you can't visit an island._
2. _____
3. _____
4. _____
5. _____
6. _____
7. _____
8. _____
9. _____

2 What can you do in Toronto?

Grammar **A** Read the guidebook. What can you do in Toronto? Complete the chart below.

TORONTO, CANADA

1. The CN Tower
Get a good view of the city from 553 meters (1,814 feet). A restaurant, shops, and a glass floor!
Hours: 10:00 a.m. to 11:00 p.m.

2. Casa Loma
Toronto's only castle.
Call for a tour.
Open 9:30 a.m. to 5:00 p.m.
(Last entry at 4:00 p.m.)

3. Yorkville
Walk around a lively historic neighborhood! Outdoor cafés, shops, and movie theaters.

4. The Art Gallery of Ontario
Hours: 10:00 a.m. to 5:30 p.m.

5. Centre Island
Take the ferry to Centre Island. Enjoy beautiful parks, great restaurants, and a children's amusement park.
Open all day.

6. Harbourfront Centre
Right on Lake Ontario, this huge center has everything for all the family. Ice skating, art, cafés, a music garden, shops, sailing, and boat tours. In the summer, there are outdoor concerts, a market, and special events.
Open from 10:00 a.m. to 9:00 p.m.

On a rainy day	On a sunny day	In the evening	With children
You can go to the Art Gallery of Ontario.			

B Complete the conversations with *can* or *can't*.

1. Jill What ____*can*____ you do at Harbourfront Centre?

   Dan Let's see . . . you _____ rent a boat. And at night, you _____ go to an outdoor concert.

   Jill Sounds great! _____ we go right now?

   Dan No, we _____ . It opens at 10:00 a.m., and it's only 7:30 a.m. now. It's really early.

   Jill Oh, you're right. Well, _____ we go to a café for breakfast?

   Dan Yes, we _____ do that. Let's go!

2. Yoshi I'm tired today. I don't want to go on another walking tour! Where _____ we go to relax?

   Keiko Let's go to Yorkville. We _____ have a nice lunch and see a movie.

   Yoshi OK, but we _____ spend a lot of money. We need to save our money for shopping!

1 What countries do you know?

Vocabulary | **A** Complete the names of the countries. Then write the countries in the chart below.

1. S _p_ ai _n_
2. ____ ____ str ____ l ____ ____
3. ____ or ____ cc ____
4. C ____ st ____ ____ ic ____
5. R ____ ss ____ ____
6. M ____ x ____ c ____

7. P ____ r ____
8. Fr ____ nc ____
9. S ____ ____ th
   K ____ r ____ ____
10. Ch ____ n ____
11. Th ____ ____ l ____ nd

12. I ____ d ____ ____
13. J ____ p ____ n
14. C ____ n ____ d ____
15. Br ____ z ____ l

I know a lot about . . .			
I don't know a lot about . . .			
They speak English in . . .			
I love the food from . . .			
I don't want to go to . . .			

B Look at the pictures. What kinds of food are these dishes? Write the nationalities.

1. _____ Japanese _____

2. _____

3. _____

4. _____

C Complete the chart.

Food I like	Food I don't like	Food I want to try	Food I can cook
Korean			French

2 Where in the world?

Vocabulary | **Complete the crossword puzzle.**

1.									
2. A	N	3. T	A	R	C	T	4. I	C	5. A
		6.							
7.				8.					
	9.								
					10.				

Across

2. There are no cities in this cold, icy region.
6. This country is in both Europe and Asia.
7. This large region includes Japan and South Korea.
9. Beijing, Shanghai, and Hong Kong are in this country.
10. This long, thin country is in South America.

Down

1. They speak both French and English in this North American country.
3. They speak this language in Turkey.
4. Rome, Venice, and Milan are cities in this European country.
5. This large country is in Oceania.
8. They speak this language in Thailand.

3 About you

Grammar | **Unscramble the questions. Then write true answers.**

1. can / sports / play / What / your best friend ?
   A _What sports can your best friend play?_
   B _____

2. food / mother / make / Can / Mexican / your ?
   A _____
   B _____

3. speak / you / languages / can / What ?
   A _____
   B _____

4. your / speak / English / parents / Can ?
   A _____
   B _____

1 What's this? What are these?

Conversation strategies | What are the things in the pictures? Write sentences. Use the words in the box.

candy   dress   drink   ✓musical instrument   sandwich   shoe

1. _It's a kind of musical_
   instrument.
   It's called an erhu.

2. _They're a kind of_
   They're called

3. _____
   _____
   _____

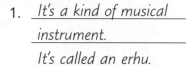

4. _____
   _____
   _____

5. _____
   _____
   _____

6. _____
   _____
   _____

2 What's an *Inukshuk*?

Conversation strategies | Complete the sentences. Then unscramble the letters from the boxes to find the answer to the question.

1. A sneaker is a kind of [s] h _o_ _e_ .
2. A *tortilla* is kind of like a _p_ ___ ___ [a] ___ ___ .
3. A *balalaika* is like a _g_ ___ ___ [t] ___ ___ .
4. *Gazpacho* is a kind of tomato _s_ ___ [ ] _p_ .
5. *Lassi* is kind of like a ___ ___ ___ _k_ _s_ ___ ___ ___ [e] .
6. Volleyball is a kind of ___ _p_ ___ _r_ [ ] .

What's an *Inukshuk*?

It's like a ___ _s_ ___ ___ _t_ ___ _e_ . You can see them in Alaska and Greenland.

3 It's a kind of pot.

Conversation strategies | Complete the conversations. Use *like*, *kind of like*, or *a kind of*.

1. A That's a beautiful dish!
   B Thanks. Actually, it's _a kind of_ pot. It's Japanese.
   A Can you cook with it? It looks so pretty.
   B Yeah! You can make Japanese food _____
      yosenabe in it.
   A Like what?
   B Yosenabe. It's _____ soup.

2. A What can you buy at the market?
   B Well, you can buy food from different countries, things
      _____ fruit. You can buy durians . . .
   A What's a durian?
   B It's _____ fruit.
   A Really?
   B Yeah. It's _____ a melon.
   A Is it good?
   B Yes, I love it.

1 FAQs about Paris

Reading **A** Read the website. Write the correct question heading for each paragraph.

Where can you eat in Paris?	✓What are great places to visit in Paris?
What do people wear in Paris?	How can I travel around Paris?

http://www.parispage...

THE PARIS PAGE

Find out all you need to know about Paris! You can <u>send your questions here</u> for other travelers to answer. Or share your information about your trip to Paris.

Frequently Asked Questions (FAQs)

What are great places to visit in Paris?

You have to see the <u>Eiffel Tower</u> on your first visit. Then go to the <u>Louvre</u>. It's a very large and famous art museum. There are also beautiful gardens near it. After that, you can visit the <u>Latin Quarter</u>. It's a very old neighborhood. It has a lot of historic buildings, museums, and great shopping. <u>More</u>

It's easy to travel in Paris. There are trains, buses, and subways. Try the subway system, called the <u>Metro</u>. There are 301 Metro stations in the city. Every building in Paris is near a Metro station, so it's very convenient, too! <u>More</u>

Parisians love food. There are amazing <u>cafés</u>, <u>bistros</u>, and other kinds of <u>restaurants</u> everywhere in the city. You can relax at an outdoor café all day. Cafés open early in the morning and usually close late in the evening. <u>More</u>

Parisians like to "dress up" and wear <u>designer clothes</u>. They don't usually wear shorts, sneakers, or T-shirts to restaurants or concerts. You can wear casual clothes and shoes in Paris, but try to look nice. <u>More</u>

<u>Next</u>

B Read the website again. Then write *T* (true) or *F* (false) for each sentence. Correct the false sentences.

1. The Louvre is a famous garden in Paris. __*F*__ *The Louvre is a famous art museum in Paris.*
2. The Latin Quarter is a historic building. ____ _____
3. The Metro is a museum in Paris. ____ _____
4. A bistro is a kind of restaurant. ____ _____
5. Cafés open late in Paris. ____ _____
6. Parisians like to wear casual clothes when they go out. ____ _____

2 FAQs about your country

Writing **A** Complete each sentence with three things about your city or country.
Make lists and use commas.

1. _El Salvador_ is famous for _its beautiful beaches, outdoor markets, and great food_ .
2. _____ is famous for _____ .
3. There are great places to see. You can visit _____ .
4. The people usually wear _____ .

B Imagine you are looking at a travel website about your country or city.
Write answers to these questions.

○○○   TRAVEL

1. I often travel there on business, but I don't usually have a lot of time. Where can I go and what can I see in one day?

   _____

   _____

   _____

2. I want to visit this summer, but I don't have a lot of money. What can I do for free?

   _____

   _____

   _____

3. Where can I meet local people? What traditional things can I see or do?

   _____

   _____

   _____

Unit 9 Progress chart

What can you do? Mark the boxes. ☑ = I can . . . ? = I need to review how to . . .	To review, go back to these pages in the Student's Book.
Grammar ☐ use *can* and *can't* to talk about things to do in a city.	86 and 87
☐ use *can* and *can't* to talk about ability.	88 and 89
Vocabulary ☐ use at least 10 new sightseeing words.	86 and 87
☐ name at least 15 countries and 5 regions.	88
☐ name at least 10 nationalities and 10 languages.	88 and 89
Conversation strategies ☐ use *a kind of* and *kind of like* to explain new words.	90
☐ use *like* to give examples.	91
Writing ☐ use commas to separate items in a list.	93

Busy lives

Lesson A — A night at home

1 What did they do last night?

Grammar | What did these people do last night? What didn't they do? Complete two sentences for each picture. Use the simple past.

stay home / visit her parents

1. Kate _stayed home_ .
   She _didn't visit her parents_ .

watch TV / practice her guitar

2. Rita _____ .
   She _____ .

study English / cook dinner

3. Mee-Sun _____ .
   She _____ .

play chess / watch a movie

4. Ali and Sam _____ .
   They _____ .

listen to music / email friends

5. Emil _____ .
   He _____ .

invite friends over / clean the house

6. Joe and Ken _____ .
   They _____ .

2 How was your weekend?

Grammar | **Complete Grace's email. Use the simple past.**

New Message

To: Paulina Lopez
From: Grace Chen
Subject: How was your weekend?

Hi Paulina!

I really _enjoyed_ (enjoy) the weekend! I _____ (invite) a friend
over on Saturday. She's my co-worker, and she's very nice. We
_____ (play) tennis in the morning and _____ (stay) at the
tennis club for lunch. Then we _____ (practice) yoga and
_____ (walk) in the park.

In the evening, we _____ (watch) a movie and _____ (cook)
a big dinner. We _____ (talk) a lot, but we _____ (not talk)
about work. And we _____ (not watch) TV all day – a nice change!

Then on Sunday, I _____ (study) English and _____ (clean) the
house. Hey! You _____ (not call) me on Sunday! Call me soon, OK?
Tell me about your weekend.

Grace

---

3 About you

Grammar
and
vocabulary | **Write true sentences about your weekend. Use the simple past. Add more information.**

1. invite a friend over   _I invited a friend over for dinner._ **or** _I didn't invite a friend over for dinner._

2. stay home   _____

3. study for an exam   _____

4. clean the house   _____

5. call a friend   _____

6. check my email   _____

7. chat online   _____

8. practice my English   _____

9. listen to music   _____

10. rent a car   _____

11. cook a big meal   _____

12. exercise   _____

Lesson B / A busy week

1 A weekly planner

Grammar and vocabulary | **Read Jenna's planner. Then complete the sentences below. Use the simple past of the verbs in the box.**

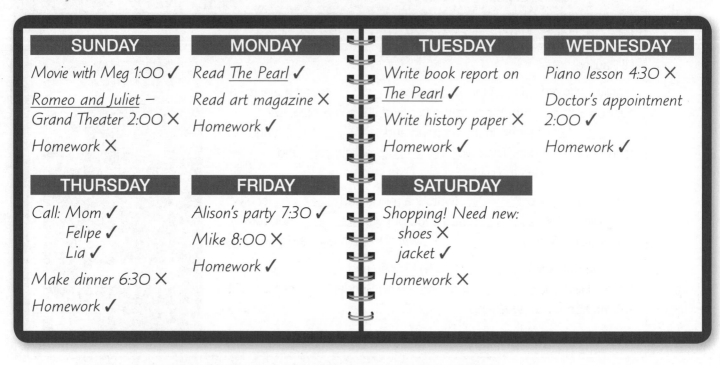

SUNDAY	MONDAY	TUESDAY	WEDNESDAY
Movie with Meg 1:00 ✓	Read _The Pearl_ ✓	Write book report on _The Pearl_ ✓	Piano lesson 4:30 ✗
Romeo and Juliet – Grand Theater 2:00 ✗	Read art magazine ✗	Write history paper ✗	Doctor's appointment 2:00 ✓
Homework ✗	Homework ✓	Homework ✓	Homework ✓

THURSDAY	FRIDAY	SATURDAY
Call: Mom ✓ Felipe ✓ Lia ✓	Alison's party 7:30 ✓	Shopping! Need new: shoes ✗ jacket ✓
Make dinner 6:30 ✗	Mike 8:00 ✗	Homework ✗
Homework ✓	Homework ✓	

| buy | do | go | have | make | read | ✓see | write |

1. On Sunday, Jenna _____*saw*_____ a movie.
   She _*didn't see*_ a play.

2. On Monday, Jenna _____ a book in English.
   She _____ a magazine.

3. Jenna _____ a book report on Tuesday.
   She _____ a history paper.

4. Jenna _____ a doctor's appointment on Wednesday.
   She _____ a piano lesson this week.

5. On Thursday, Jenna _____ a lot of phone calls.
   She _____ dinner.

6. On Friday, Jenna _____ to a party.
   She _____ out with Mike.

7. Jenna _____ a new jacket on Saturday.
   She _____ new shoes.

8. Jenna _____ homework every school day.
   She _____ homework on the weekend.

About you

Grammar and vocabulary **A** Complete the questions in the questionnaire. Use the simple past of the verbs in the box. Then write true answers. Write more than *yes* or *no*.

do	eat	✓go	have	make	see	speak	take	write

QUESTIONNAIRE: Did you . . . ?

1. __*Did*__ you __*go*__ out a lot last week?
   Yes, I did. I went out every night last week. **or** *No, I didn't. I stayed home.*

2. _____ you and your family _____ dinner in front of the TV last night?
   _____

3. _____ you _____ anything interesting last weekend?
   _____

4. _____ you _____ in a restaurant on Friday night?
   _____

5. _____ your class _____ a test or an exam last week?
   _____

6. _____ you _____ dinner every night last week?
   _____

7. _____ your best friend _____ you an email yesterday?
   _____

8. _____ your parents _____ a movie on Saturday night?
   _____

9. _____ you _____ to a lot of friends in class yesterday?
   _____

B Write a sentence about each day last week. Write one thing you did each day.

1. Monday _____
2. Tuesday _____
3. Wednesday _____
4. Thursday _____
5. Friday _____
6. Saturday _____
7. Sunday _____

1 Responding to news

Conversation strategies **A** Complete the conversations. Circle and write the best response.

1. A   I bought a new TV today.

    B   _Good for you!_

    (a.) Good for you!

    b. I'm sorry to hear that.

    c. Good luck!

2. A   I'm 25 today!

    B   _____

    a. I'm sorry to hear that.

    b. Good luck!

    c. Happy birthday!

3. A   My wife had a baby girl last night.

    B   _____

    a. Good for you!

    b. Happy birthday!

    c. Congratulations!

4. A   I have a job interview today.

    B   _____

    a. I'm sorry to hear that.

    b. Good luck!

    c. Happy birthday!

5. A   I finally passed my English exam.

    B   _____

    a. Thank goodness!

    b. I'm sorry to hear that.

    c. Good luck!

6. A   I didn't get the job I wanted.

    B   _____

    a. I'm sorry to hear that.

    b. Thank goodness!

    c. Good for you!

B Your friend tells you some news, and you respond. Write the conversations.

1. Your friend bought a new car, and he got a bargain.

    I bought a new car today. I got a bargain.   _Good for you!_

2. Your friend got 100% on her English exam.

3. Your friend finally got a job.

4. Your friend wanted to go on vacation, but he has no money.

2 You did?

Conversation strategies **A** Complete the conversations with the expressions in the box.

✓You did?   You did?   You did?   Good luck!   I'm sorry to hear that.   Good for you.

1. **Lilly** Did you have a busy day?

   Beth Yeah, I'm exhausted. I went shopping downtown.

   Lilly ___You___ ___did?___ Did you buy anything?

   Beth Yes, I bought a new suit. And a blouse and shoes.

   Lilly _____ _____ _____

   Beth And then I had lunch with Maria, and we talked all
   afternoon. How about you?

   Lilly I cleaned the house, did the laundry, and made dinner.

   Beth _____ _____ That's great! I'm starving! Let's eat!

2. **Jun** Did you have a good week?

   José Actually, no. I had five exams.

   Jun _____ _____ That's awful. Did you pass?

   José Well, I passed three and failed two.

   Jun Oh. _____ _____ _____ _____ _____

   José And I have two exams tomorrow, too.

   Jun _____ _____ Study hard!

B Write two responses for each piece of news.

1. I had a terrible vacation in Hawaii.

   You did? _I'm sorry to hear that._

2. I took my driver's test yesterday.

   _____ _____

3. I wrote an article for a magazine last month.

   _____ _____

4. My friend and I worked all weekend.

   _____ _____

1 A busy birthday . . .

Reading | **A** Look at the four pictures. Then read Peter's blog. Number the pictures in order from 1 to 4.

Friday, May 28 11:45 p.m.

I had a crazy day today. I had an English exam, and it's my birthday!

I had the exam at 8:30 this morning. I needed to study, so I woke up early – at 6:30 a.m. I took a shower, made some coffee, and studied for about an hour. Well, the coffee didn't work. I fell asleep!
I woke up at 8:20 with my head on my books. I had ten minutes before the test started!

I ran outside, got on my bike, and went to English class. I got there right at 8:30, but guess what! The teacher never came! My classmates and I waited about half an hour. Then we left. It's great. Now I can really study for the exam.

I had breakfast, and then I went to my next class – math. ☹ I think math is really hard, but I have to take it. My teacher talked for an hour. I wanted to write some notes, but I fell asleep. I need to borrow my friend's notes.

After I finished class, I met my friend Louisa, and we went to a movie together. It was my birthday, so she paid! Great! We saw a new romantic drama. You know, I usually like drama movies a lot, but I didn't like that movie very much.

When I got home from the movie, my mother called and sang "Happy Birthday" to me. Now I have to stay up and finish a paper for a class tomorrow. I hope I don't fall asleep again!

Posted by Peter Miller

0 comments

B Read the blog again. Then answer the questions. Give reasons for the answers.

1. Did Peter get up late? _No, he didn't. He needed to study._

2. Did Peter take an English exam? _____

3. Did he listen to his math teacher? _____

4. Did he go out with a friend? _____

5. Did Peter's mother call? _____

6. Do you think he's a good student? _____

2 My last birthday

A Read the blog on page 80 again. Match the two parts of each sentence.

1. Peter studied when __c__

2. Peter had breakfast after _____

3. When Peter went to his math class, _____

4. Peter finished classes. Then _____

5. Peter saw a movie before _____

a. he went home.

b. he fell asleep again.

✓ c. he got up in the morning.

d. he met his friend Louisa.

e. he left his English class.

B Think about a day you remember well. Answer these questions. Write more than *yes* or *no*.

1. Did you work or have classes? _____

2. Did you go out with friends? _____

3. Did you do something fun? _____

4. Did you eat any of your favorite foods? _____

5. Did you go to any stores? _____

6. Did you get home late? _____

C Write a paragraph for your own blog. Use your ideas from part B.
Use *before*, *after*, *when*, or *then*, if possible.

I remember my last birthday. I _____

_____

_____

_____

_____

Unit 10 Progress chart

What can you do? Mark the boxes. ✓ = I can . . . ? = I need to review how to . . .	To review, go back to these pages in the Student's Book.
Grammar ☐ make simple past statements with regular verbs.	98 and 99
☐ make simple past statements with irregular verbs.	100 and 101
☐ ask simple past *yes-no* questions.	101
Vocabulary ☐ make simple past forms of at least 12 regular verbs.	98 and 99
☐ make simple past forms of at least 8 irregular verbs.	100 and 101
☐ use time expressions with the simple past.	101
Conversation strategies ☐ use responses like *Good for you!* and *Congratulations!*	102 and 103
☐ use *You did?* to show I'm listening, surprised, or interested.	103
Writing ☐ use *before*, *after*, *when*, and *then* to order events.	105

1 Yesterday

Vocabulary | Complete the sentences. Use the words in the box.

| busy | ✓ happy | nervous | nice | quiet | scared |

1. Yesterday was my birthday. My friends had a party for me, and I got a lot of presents. I was very __*happy*__ .
2. My family and I live in a very small town. There are no clubs or movie theaters. My town is really _____ – especially at night.
3. I started a new job yesterday. I was really _____ of my new boss.
4. I had a lot of things to do yesterday. I was pretty _____ .
5. My best friend's parents are friendly. They're very _____ .
6. We had a French test last week. I was really _____ , but I passed.

2 It was fun!

Vocabulary | Choose the best two words to complete each sentence. Cross out the wrong word.

I remember my first driving lesson. Before I met the teacher, I was really ~~scary~~ / **nervous** / **scared**. But then I relaxed because he was very **nice** / **strict** / **friendly**. The lesson was **awful** / **good** / **fun** because I didn't make a lot of mistakes. I was pretty good. At the end of the lesson, I was **exhausted** / **lazy** / **tired**. It was hard work! After ten lessons, I took my test, but I didn't pass. I wasn't **awful** / **pleased** / **happy**. But I passed three weeks later. Now I can drive my dad's **nice** / **new** / **awful** car.

3 I remember . . .

Grammar | **Complete the conversations with *was, wasn't, were,* or *weren't*.**

1. Sally Do you remember your first date, Grandpa?

    Grandpa Yes. I ___*was*___ 16, and the girl _____ in my class.

    We _____ classmates. We went to the movies.

    Sally _____ you nervous?

    Grandpa No, I _____ . It _____ a lot of fun.

    Sally Do you remember her name?

    Grandpa Yes. Grandma!

2. Paula I remember my first day of high school.

    It _____ a hot day, and I went with

    two of my friends.

    Kenton _____ you scared?

    Paula No, we _____ really scared, but I

    guess we _____ a little nervous.

    Kenton _____ the teachers friendly?

    Paula Yes, they _____ very nice.

    Thank goodness.

3. Sun-Hee Do you remember your first college English class?

    Carla Yes, it _____ last year. I _____ very good at

    English, and I made a lot of mistakes. My partner's

    English _____ very good, so he _____

    very happy with me!

    Sun-Hee _____ he smart? I mean, intelligent?

    Carla Yes, he _____ .

    Sun-Hee So, was your first class fun?

    Carla No, it _____ . In fact,

    it _____ awful.

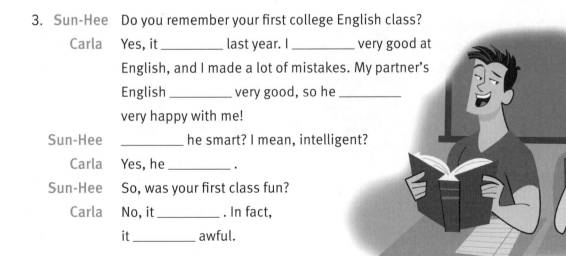

1 About you

Grammar and vocabulary | **A** **Unscramble the questions. Then write true answers.**

1. trip or vacation / was / last / your / When ?

   A _When was your last trip or vacation?_

   B _____

2. go / did / Where / exactly / you ?

   A _____

   B _____

3. weather / like / was / the / What ?

   A _____

   B _____

4. you / there / do / did / What ?

   A _____

   B _____

5. were / there / How / you / long ?

   A _____

   B _____

Grammar | **B** **Read about Emi's first trip to the park with a friend. Write questions for the answers.**

"We weren't very old – I think I was eight, and my friend was ten. We went to the park, but my mother didn't know. We had a great time! We went swimming in the pool. I remember it was a beautiful day – warm and sunny. We were there about an hour. Then we got hungry, so we went home. When we got back, my mother wasn't too happy."

1. A _How old was Emi?_

   B Eight.

2. A _____

   B To the park.

3. A _____

   B Her friend.

4. A _____

   B They went swimming.

5. A _____

   B Warm and sunny.

6. A _____

   B About an hour.

2 Get and go

Vocabulary | **A** Which of these expressions do you use with *get*? Which do you use with *go*? Which can you use with *get* and *go*? Complete the chart.

✓ back	to bed	scared	swimming	to the movies	a view of something
✓ lost	a gift	skiing	(an) autograph	snorkeling	along with someone
home	hiking	camping	on vacation	a bad sunburn	to see a concert / movie
sick	biking	married	up early or late	on a road trip	to the beach

get	go	get and go
lost		back

B Complete the questions with *get* or *go*. Then write your own answers.

1. A What time do you ___*go* **or** *get*___ to bed on weeknights?

   B _____

2. A How often do you _____ swimming?

   B _____

3. A Did you _____ a bad sunburn last year?

   B _____

4. A What did you _____ for your last birthday?

   B _____

5. A Can you think of someone you don't _____ along with?

   B _____

6. A Where do you want to _____ on vacation this year?

   B _____

7. A Do you _____ up early in the morning?

   B _____

1 Asking questions

Conversation strategies | Complete each conversation with two questions.

1. **Sadie** How was your weekend?

   Bill It was awful. We went hang gliding. I hated it!

   Sadie That's too bad.

   Bill Yeah. Anyway, how about you?

   What did you do?

   Did you do anything special?

   Sadie Well, we rented a car and went camping.

   Bill That sounds nice.

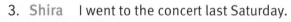

2. **Dirk** Did you go out last night?

   Leo Yeah, I met a friend and went to a club.

   _____

   _____

   Dirk Oh, I went to the laundromat and did my laundry. I didn't do anything exciting.

3. **Shira** I went to the concert last Saturday.

   Jaz I did, too! The band sounded great.

   _____

   _____

   Shira Oh, it was fantastic. Well, anyway, it's 11:30.

   Jaz Yeah, it's late. See you tomorrow.

4. **Gabor** So, did you work last weekend?

   Koji Yeah, Saturday and Sunday. We were really busy.

   _____

   _____

   Gabor Let's see . . . I went shopping, um, and saw a movie. Then on Sunday, I played tennis, made dinner, . . .

   Koji I guess you were busy, too!

2 Well, anyway, . . .

Conversation
strategies **A** Use *anyway* three times in this conversation. Leave two of the blanks empty.

Mirka   Where were you last week? Were you away?

Arlen   Yes, I was in Mexico on business.

Mirka   Mexico? What was that like?

Arlen   Oh, great. The customers there are really nice.
_____ I always enjoy my trips to Mexico.
The people are so friendly.

Mirka   That's nice. _____ So you're traveling a
lot these days.

Arlen   Yeah. About six times a year. _____ ,
what about you? Did you have a good week?

Mirka   Not bad. I had a lot of meetings – you know, the
usual. _____ , do you want to go out
tonight? We can have dinner maybe.

Arlen   Sure. We can meet after work.

Mirka   OK. Well, _____ , I have to go. See you later.

B Use the instructions to complete the conversations.

1. Friend   What do you usually do on the weekends?

   You   *I usually go out with friends. What about you?*
   (Answer. Then ask a question about your friend.)

   Friend   Me? I usually go to see a movie. Sometimes a friend and I go camping or hiking.

2. Friend   I'm enjoying my new job. My boss is OK, and the people are nice. We get
   along – it's a friendly place.

   You   That's nice. _____
   (Change the topic. Invite your friend for dinner tomorrow.)

   Friend   Tomorrow? Sounds great. What time? Seven?

3. Friend   What did you do for your last birthday?

   You   _____
   (Answer. Then end the conversation. It's late.)

   Friend   OK. Talk to you later.

4. Friend   So how was your weekend?

   You   _____
   (Answer. Then change the topic. Invite your friend to do something fun next weekend.)

   Friend   Sure. Sounds like fun.

1 My first job

Reading **A** Read the story. What are these people like? Match the names with the adjectives.

1. Diana ___a___   ✓ a. friendly
2. Joe _____   b. nervous
3. Megan _____   c. good looking
4. Rick _____   d. strict

Tell Us About Your First Job

Reader Megan Walker writes in with a story about her first job.

I remember my first job. I worked in an outdoor café one summer. It was called Sunny's. I got free drinks and food. My boss Diana was very friendly, and I got along well with her. Her husband Joe worked there, too, but he was really strict. On my first day, I was late because I got lost on the subway. After that, Joe was never too happy with me.

So, every day I served sandwiches and coffee. The café was really busy all the time. I wasn't a very good server, so I was often nervous. Also, I was always exhausted by the end of the day.

One day, I was really tired, so I asked to go home early. Joe looked angry, but he said, "OK. Fine." I left and went to the subway.

Then I met my friend Rick on the street. He was really good looking, and I liked him a lot. He said, "Do you want to go and eat something?" I said, "Yes. OK. Where?" And he said, "I know a café near here. Let's go there. They have good sandwiches."

So we went back to Sunny's and sat down to eat! We waited for about ten minutes before Joe finally came over to the table. He was very busy, so he didn't look at me. He said, "I'm sorry. One of the servers left early. Are you ready to order?" We stayed for an hour. I was lucky because my boss never saw me, but I had to pay for my sandwich and soda!

– Megan Walker
New York City

B Read Megan's story again. Then answer the questions.

1. Where did Megan work? _She worked at Sunny's._

2. How did Megan get to work? _____

3. What kind of food did she serve? _____

4. What was the café like? _____

5. Why did she leave early one day? _____

6. Why did she go back to Sunny's? _____

7. How long did they stay at Sunny's? _____

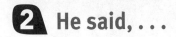 **He said, . . .**

A   Read the rest of the story. Rewrite their conversation after they leave the café. Use quoted speech. Add capital letters and correct punctuation (" " , . ?).

Rick and I left the café and talked for a few minutes.

rick asked how did you like the café   _Rick asked, "How did you like the café?"_

I said it's nice   _____

he said the service wasn't very good   _____

I said well one of the servers left early   _____

rick said people are so lazy these days   _____

I said yes I know   _____

But I didn't tell Rick I was the server!

B   Think about a time you met a friend for the first time. Answer these questions.

1.   How old were you?   _____

2.   What was your friend's name?   _____

3.   How did you first meet? What happened?   _____

4.   What did you say when you first met? I said, "_____."

5.   What did your friend say? She / He said, "_____."

C   Now write a story about meeting your friend. Use your ideas from part B.

When we met, I was 13 and _____ . _____

_____

_____

_____

Unit 11 Progress chart

What can you do? Mark the boxes. ✓ = I can . . . ? = I need to review how to . . .	To review, go back to these pages in the Student's Book.
Grammar ☐ make simple past statements and questions with *be*.	108 and 109
☐ ask simple past information questions.	110
Vocabulary ☐ name at least 12 words to describe people or experiences.	108 and 109
☐ name at least 4 new expressions with *go*.	111
☐ name at least 5 new expressions with *get*.	111
Conversation strategies ☐ ask and answer questions to show interest.	112
☐ use *Anyway* to change the topic or end a conversation.	113
Writing ☐ use capitals and punctuation in quoted speech.	115

Fabulous food

Lesson A — Eating habits

1 Mmmmm!

Vocabulary | Write the names of the foods. Then find the words in the puzzle. Look in these directions (→↓).

1. _meat_

2. _seafood_

3. _____

4. _____

5. _____

6. _____

7. _____

8. _____

9. _____

10. _____

11. _____

12. _____

13. _____

14. _____

15. _____

16. _____

17. _____

18. _____

F	F	V	C	A	R	R	O	T	S
R	X	E	B	I	B	E	E	F	S
U	O	G	A	X	R	M	E	A	T
I	A	E	N	S	E	I	S	T	A
T	E	T	A	E	A	L	L	C	E
G	G	A	N	A	D	K	F	H	P
P	G	B	A	F	R	U	I	E	P
O	S	L	S	O	P	P	D	E	A
T	F	E	N	O	U	D	L	S	S
A	I	S	Z	D	I	H	G	E	T
T	S	H	R	I	C	E	F	Q	A
O	H	C	H	I	C	K	E	N	M
E	C	U	C	U	M	B	E	R	S
S	H	E	L	L	F	I	S	H	Z

2 An invitation to dinner

Grammar | **A** Read the invitation. Then circle the correct words to complete the emails.

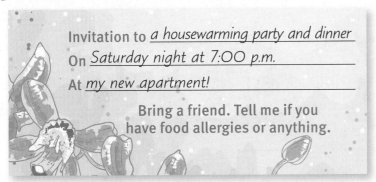

Invitation to *a housewarming party and dinner*
On *Saturday night at 7:00 p.m.*
At *my new apartment!*

Bring a friend. Tell me if you
have food allergies or anything.

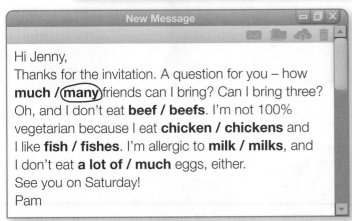

New Message

Hi Jenny,
Thanks for the invitation. A question for you – how
much /(many) friends can I bring? Can I bring three?
Oh, and I don't eat **beef / beefs**. I'm not 100%
vegetarian because I eat **chicken / chickens** and
I like **fish / fishes**. I'm allergic to **milk / milks**, and
I don't eat **a lot of / much** eggs, either.
See you on Saturday!
Pam

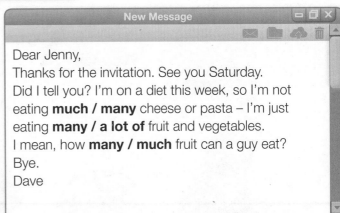

New Message

Dear Jenny,
Thanks for the invitation. See you Saturday.
Did I tell you? I'm on a diet this week, so I'm not
eating **much / many** cheese or pasta – I'm just
eating **many / a lot of** fruit and vegetables.
I mean, how **many / much** fruit can a guy eat?
Bye.
Dave

B Write your own email to Jenny. Tell her about these foods.

- food you like
- food you don't like
- food you eat a lot of
- food you don't eat a lot of

New Message

Dear Jenny,
Thanks for the invitation to the party. _____
_____
_____
_____
_____
_____

3 About you

Grammar
and
vocabulary | Complete the questions with *How much* or *How many*. Then write your own answers.

1. _*How many*_ students in your class are vegetarians? _____
2. _____ milk does your family buy every week? _____
3. _____ times a week do you eat chicken? _____
4. _____ shellfish do you eat? Do you eat a lot? _____
5. _____ of your friends are picky eaters? _____
6. _____ cans of soda do you drink a day? _____

1 At the supermarket

Vocabulary | Write the words under the pictures. Then write the food in the chart below.

 1. _apples_

 2. _____

 3. _____

 4. _____

 5. _____

 6. _____

 7. _____

 8. _____

 9. _____

 10. _____

 11. _____

 12. _____

 13. _____

 14. _____

 15. _____

 16. _____

 17. _____

 18. _____

 19. _____

20. _____

meat and seafood	fruit	vegetables	other
	apples		

2 What would you like?

Grammar | **Complete the conversations. Use *would you like* or *'d like*.**

1. Jim What _would you like_ ?

   Megan I _____ ice cream, please.
   Jim _____ chocolate sprinkles?
   Megan Yes, please.

2. Server Good evening. _____ something to drink?

   Dan Oh, just water, please.
   Server OK. And what _____ to eat?
   Dan Um, I _____ the salmon, please.
   Server _____ some green beans with it?
   Dan Actually, I _____ some spinach, please.

3. Greg Where _____ to go for dinner?

   Sheila Oh, I don't know. I _____ to go
   somewhere around here.
   Greg _____ to try the new Thai restaurant?
   Sheila Oh, yes! I _____ something spicy.

3 *Some* or *any*

Grammar | **Complete the conversations with *some* or *any*.**

1. Ming Polly, try _some_ lamb.
   Polly Gosh, it's hot! I need _____ water . . . now!
   Ming Here. Drink _____ soda.

2. John Do you have _____ chocolate cookies?

   Ken No, but we have _____ peanut butter cookies.
   John OK, I'll take _____ .

3. Sara Would you like _____ potato chips?
   Craig Yeah, but I don't have _____ money.
   Sara Oh, and I don't have _____ , either.

1 Something for lunch

Complete the conversation with *or something* or *or anything*.

Trish Do you go out for lunch every day or . . . ?

Pete Well, I don't usually eat lunch. I don't like to eat a big meal _or anything_ at lunchtime.

Trish No? You don't have a snack _____ ?

Pete Well, I sometimes have a hot drink, like hot chocolate _____ .

Trish Well, I'm hungry – I'd like a sandwich _____ . Would you like something to eat?

Pete Well, maybe . . .

Trish How about a salad _____ ?

Pete Yes, OK. Actually, I'd like a chicken sandwich. Oh, let's get some ice cream _____ , too. I guess I *am* hungry!

2 About you

Answer the questions. Write true answers. Use *or something* or *or anything*.

1. Are you a picky eater? *Well, I don't eat fish or shrimp or anything.*

2. What do you usually have for dinner? _____

3. How about lunch? _____

4. What do you like to order in restaurants? _____

5. What do you drink with meals? _____

6. What kinds of snacks do you like? _____

❸ Would you like to go out or . . . ?

Complete the conversations. Which questions can end with *or* . . . ? Add *or* . . . where possible.

1. Paul What would you like for dinner tonight _____ ?
   Would you like to go out <u>*or* . . .</u> ?

   Val Yes, please! I'd love to eat out.

   Paul That's great. So can I choose the restaurant _____ ?

   Val Sure.

   Paul Let's see . . . would you like a pizza _____ ?

   Val Um, I don't want Italian tonight. How about an Asian place? Do you like Korean or Thai _____ ?

   Paul Uh, I don't really care for spicy food.

   Val Let me think . . . do you want to get a hamburger _____ ?

   Paul Yeah! With maybe some French fries and some cookies.

   Val OK! Stop! I'm starving! Let's go!

2. Kate It's my birthday today.

   Sally Happy birthday! Do you have plans _____ ?

   Kate I had plans, but my friend just called. He's sick.

   Sally That's terrible! I know. Let's eat at my house. I can cook some steaks or something. What do you think _____ ?

   Kate That's very nice, thanks, but I'm a vegetarian.

   Sally Oh. Do you eat pasta _____ ?

   Kate Well, I can't eat pasta or anything heavy right now. I'm on a diet.

   Sally OK. No pasta. What would you like _____ ?

   Kate Do you have any fruit _____ ?

   Sally Sorry. I ate the last banana this morning before I went to work. I have some carrots. . . .

   Kate Let's stop at the supermarket on our way to your house.

1 Healthy fast food

Reading | **A** Read the blog post. Find the answers to these questions.

1. Where did the writer eat breakfast? _____
2. What breakfast food does the writer recommend? _____
3. How many calories were in the writer's lunch? _____

TASTES GOOD, AND GOOD FOR YOU!

We often think of fast food as hamburgers, fried chicken, hot dogs, and French fries. However, some fast-food restaurants are starting to offer healthy foods, too. But how healthy is "healthy" fast-food, and how does it taste? I went to some famous fast-food restaurants last week to find the answer and was pleasantly surprised. Here are the two healthy fast-food choices I recommend.

BURGER RESTAURANTS: OATMEAL, PLEASE!

Many burger restaurants open early and serve breakfast, too. One popular restaurant chain has a breakfast with more than 1,000 calories. That's about half the calories you need for a whole day! For a healthy option, you can now choose apple slices (15 calories), fruit and nuts (210 calories), or oatmeal (290 calories). I tried the oatmeal, and it was delicious!

MEXICAN RESTAURANTS: I'D LIKE IT IN A BOWL

I love Mexican fast food as a special treat, but I'm pleased to see that my favorite taco restaurant now has a lot of healthy choices on the menu. A taco salad with beef and cheese is about 600 calories. However, I went for chicken. You can make your own meal with chicken, rice, tomatoes, and other healthy foods. I tried it for lunch. I got it in a bowl and said no to the tortilla chips. It was very tasty and only 450 calories.

Do you know any great, healthy fast-food places? Tell us in the comments section.

B Read the blog post again. Then choose the correct words to complete these sentences.

1. The writer wanted to try some **hamburgers / healthy food** last week.
2. He thinks that 1,000 calories **is / is not** a lot for breakfast.
3. He **enjoyed / didn't enjoy** the oatmeal.
4. He had **taco salad / chicken** for lunch.
5. He **ate / didn't eat** tortilla chips with his lunch.
6. His lunch was **very / not very** healthy.

2 Restaurant reviews

Writing | **A** Jill Heacock is a restaurant reviewer. She ate at the Seafood Palace last week, and she loved it. Circle the correct words to complete Jill's review.

THIS WEEK'S RESTAURANT: **THE SEAFOOD PALACE**　　　★ ★ ★ ★

by Jill Heacock

　　Last week, I went to the Seafood Palace – it's a **terrible /** (**wonderful**) restaurant. I loved it. I was there on a busy night, and the atmosphere was **fun / formal**. The food was **awful / delicious**, and every dish came to the table **cold / hot**. I really liked the shrimp. Very tasty! The service was **excellent / slow**, the servers were really **friendly / lazy**, and the meal was **cheap / expensive**. I only spent $12!

　　The Seafood Palace is a good place to hang out with friends or have dinner with your family. Try it!

B Imagine you are a restaurant reviewer. You ate at a restaurant, and you hated it. Write your review.

THIS WEEK'S RESTAURANT: _____　　　★

by _____

　　Last week, I went to _____ – it's a terrible restaurant! _____

_____

_____

_____

_____

_____

Unit 12 Progress chart

What can you do? Mark the boxes. ✓ = I can . . .　　　? = I need to review how to . . .	To review, go back to these pages in the Student's Book.
Grammar	
☐ use countable and uncountable nouns.	118 and 119
☐ make statements and questions with *much, many,* and *a lot of.*	118 and 119
☐ make statements and questions with *some, any,* and *not any.*	120 and 121
☐ make offers and requests with *would like.*	121
Vocabulary	
☐ name at least 5 categories of food.	118 and 119
☐ name at least 25 different foods.	118, 119, and 120
Conversation strategies	
☐ use *or something* and *or anything.*	122
☐ use *or . . . ?* in *yes-no* questions to make them less direct.	123
Writing	
☐ use expressions to talk about restaurants.	124 and 125

Illustration credits

Ken Batelman: 42   **Harry Briggs:** 15, 61 *(4 at bottom)*, 69   **Domninic Bugatto:** 8, 23, 27, 38, 59, 78   **Cambridge University Press:** 67
Matt Collins: 22, 54   **Chuck Gonzales:** 5, 11, 26, 45, 80   **Cheryl Hoffman:** 3, 24, 47, 61 *(2 at top)*   **Jon Keegan:** 19, 51, 94, 95
Frank Montagna: 2, 13, 21, 53, 82, 83   **Greg White:** 7, 16, 37, 79   **Terry Wong:** 30, 46, 63, 74, 86   **Filip Yip:** 70

Photo credits

3 *(clockwise from top left)* ©Exactostock/SuperStock; ©Elea Dumas/Getty Images; ©MIXA/Getty Images; ©Thinkstock   **4** ©Ryan McVay/Getty Images   **7** ©wavebreakmedia/Shutterstock   **10** *(clockwise from top left)* ©Andresr/Shutterstock; ©MTPA Stock/Masterfile; ©Spencer Grant/PhotoEdit; ©Jose Luiz Pelaez Inc./Corbis; ©Medioimages/Photodisc/Thinkstock; ©Terry Doyle/Getty Images   **11** *(top to bottom)* ©Image Source/SuperStock; ©kurhan/Shutterstock   **12** *(pen)* ©Phant/Shutterstock; *(potato chips)* ©Thinkstock; *(wallet)* ©AlexTois/Shutterstock; *(laptop)* ©Alex Staroseltsev/Shutterstock; *(umbrella)* ©K. Miri Photography/Shutterstock; *(bag)* ©Hemera Technologies/Thinkstock; *(glasses)* ©Ingvar Bjork/Shutterstock; *(keys)* ©SELEZNEV VALERY/Shutterstock; *(notebook)* ©zirconicusso/Shutterstock; *(smartphone)* ©Oleksiy Mark/Shutterstock; *(water bottle)* ©lucadp/Shutterstock; *(eraser)* ©GreenStockCreative/Shutterstock; *(watch)* ©Venus Angel/Shutterstock; *(butterfly Hunter/Shutterstock; (pencil)* ©Julia Ivantsova/Shutterstock; *(hand holding smartphone)* ©Thinkstock; *(hand holding water bottle)* ©DenisNata/Shutterstock; *(all others)* ©George Kerrigan   **14** *(top row, left to right)* ©Rtimages/Shutterstock; ©Cambridge University Press; ©Thinkstock; ©Cambridge University Press *(middle row, left to right)* ©Ryan McVay/Thinkstock; ©Ryan McVay/Thinkstock; ©Thinkstock; ©Pixtal/age Fotostock *(bottom row, left to right)* ©Cambridge University Press; ©Cambridge University Press; ©Photodisc/Thinkstock; ©vovan/Shutterstock   **19** ©Design Pics/SuperStock   **20** *(clockwise from top left)* ©Exactostock/SuperStock; ©Exactostock/SuperStock; ©Mark Scott/Getty Images; ©Fancy Collection/SuperStock; ©Andreas Pollok/Getty Images; ©Ron Chapple/Getty Images; ©rSnapshotPhotos/Shutterstock; ©Peter Cade/Getty Images   **28** ©Don Nichols/Getty Images   **29** *(top to bottom)* ©Larry Dale Gordon/Getty Image; ©Punchstock   **32** *(television)* ©Maxx-Studio/Shutterstock   **35** *(top to bottom)* ©Darren Mower/Getty Images; ©Thinkstock   **36** *(top row, left to right)* ©JOSE LUIS SALMERON Notimex/Newscom; ©The Everett Collection; ©The Everett Collection; ©Getty Images *(bottom row, left to right)* ©Lions Gate/courtesy Everett Collection; ©Eric Roberts/Corbis; ©Robert Voets/CBS via Getty Images; ©Ann Johansson/Corbis   **40** ©violetblue/Shutterstock   **43** *(left to right)* ©Maxx-Studio/Shutterstock; ©MariusdeGraf/Shutterstock   **44** *(clockwise from top left)* ©Cambridge University Press; ©Artur Synenko/Shutterstock; ©Cambridge University Press; ©Cambridge University Press; ©Cambridge University Press; ©Cambridge University Press   **45** ©Punchstock   **47** ©Anders Blomqvist/Getty Images   **48** *(left to right)* ©Ambient Images Inc./Alamy; ©Yellow Dog Productions/Getty Images; ©Spencer Grant/PhotoEdit; ©David Grossman/Imageworks   **50** *(clockwise from top left)* ©Holly Harris/Getty Images; © Kwame Zikomo/SuperStock; © Jens Lucking/Getty Image; © Kaz Chiba/Getty Images; © Onoky/SuperStock; © I. Hatz/Masterfile   **52** *(top row, all photos)* ©Cambridge University Press *(middle row, left to right)* ©Cambridge University Press; ©Rudy Umans/Shutterstock; ©JupiterImages *(bottom row, left to right)* ©JupiterImages; ©Cambridge University Press; ©Danilo Calilung/Corbis   **56** ©Mike Powell/Getty Images   **58** *(sweater)* ©Karina Bakalyan/Shutterstock; *(skirt)* ©Ruslan Kudrin/Shutterstock; *(jeans)* ©Karkas/Shutterstock *(all others)* ©Cambridge University Press   **60** ©George Kerrigan   **64** *(clockwise from top left)* ©Belinda Images/SuperStock; ©Ingram Publishing/SuperStock; ©Blend Images/SuperStock; ©Punchstock *(mouse)* ©urfin/Shutterstock   **66** *(top row, left to right)* ©Catherine Karnow/Corbis; ©Shawn Baldwin/EPA/Newscom; ©Fotosonline/Alamy *(middle row, left to right)* ©Peter Willi/SuperStock; ©Douglas Pulsipher/Alamy; ©KSTFoto/Alamy *(bottom row, left to right)* ©Cambridge University Press; ©Prisma Bildagentur AG/Alamy; ©S.T. Yiap Still Life/Alamy   **67** *(top to bottom)* ©Bob Krist/Corbis; ©Ron Erwin/Getty Images; ©Bert Hoferichter/Alamy   **68** *(clockwise from top left)* ©Enzo/agefotostock; ©Olga Lyubkina/Shutterstock; ©Olga Miltsova/Shutterstock; ©Joseph Dilag/Shutterstock   **69** ©Steve Hix/Somos Images/Corbis   **71** *(top to bottom)* ©Laura Coles/Getty Images; ©Datacraft Co Ltd/Getty Images; ©panda3800/Shutterstock   **72** *(top to bottom)* ©Stephen Johnson/Getty Images; ©Simon DesRochers/Masterfile; ©ImagesEurope/Alamy; ©David Robinson/Snap2000 Images/Alamy **75** © Best View Stock/Alamy   **76** ©Thinkstock   **82** ©Thinkstock   **84** *(top to bottom)* ©Exactostock/SuperStock; ©Joe McBride/Getty Images   **85** ©David Young-Wolff/PhotoEdit   **87** ©Blend Images/SuperStock   **90** *(clockwise from top left)* ©Cambridge University Press; ©Alexander Raths/Shutterstock; ©Cambridge University Press; ©Africa Studio/Shutterstock; ©Cambridge University Press; ©Cambridge University Press; ©Cambridge University Press; ©Cambridge University Press; ©Lepas/Shutterstock; ©Luis Carlos Jimenez del rio/Shutterstock; ©Jonelle Weaver/Getty Images; ©Cambridge University Press; ©Tetra Images/SuperStock; ©Cambridge University Press; ©Nixx Photography/Shutterstock; ©Orange Stock Photo Production Inc./Alamy; ©simpleman/Shutterstock   **91** ©jet/Shutterstock   **92** *(top row, left to right)* ©Cambridge University Press; ©Cambridge University Press; ©Cambridge University Press; ©Thinkstock; ©Cambridge University Press *(top middle row, left to right)* ©Ryan McVay/Thinkstock; ©Valentyn Volkov/Shutterstock; ©Thinkstock; ©Cambridge University Press; ©Cambridge University Press *(bottom middle row, left to right)* ©Cambridge University Press; ©Cambridge University Press; ©Cambridge University Press; ©Cambridge University Press; ©Multiart/Shutterstock *(bottom row, left to right)* ©Cambridge University Press; ©Cambridge University Press; ©Cambridge University Press; ©Cambridge University Press; ©svry/Shutterstock   **93** *(top to bottom)* ©Cambridge University Press; ©Thinkstock; ©Thinkstock; ©Fuse/Getty Images/RF   **96** ©Lena Pantiukh/Shutterstock

Text credits

While every effort has been made, it has not always been possible to identify the sources of all the material used, or to trace all copyright holders. If any omissions are brought to our notice, we will be happy to include the appropriate acknowledgements on reprinting.

Special thanks to Kerry S. Vrabel for his editorial contributions.

TOUCHSTONE

JANET GOKAY

SERIES AUTHORS

MICHAEL McCARTHY

JEANNE McCARTEN

HELEN SANDIFORD

VIDEO ACTIVITY PAGES

CAMBRIDGE
UNIVERSITY PRESS

Contents

Character descriptions

Touchstone Video is a fun-filled, compelling situational comedy featuring a group of young people who are friends. David Parker is a reporter. His roommate is Alex Santos, a personal trainer. David's friend Gio Ferrari is a student visiting from Italy. Liz Martin is a singer and Web designer. She lives with Yoko Suzuki, a chef. Kim Davis is David's co-worker. She works in an office.

Through the daily encounters and activities of these characters, you have the opportunity to see and hear the language of the Student's Book vividly come to life in circumstances both familiar and entertaining.

This is David Parker.
He's a reporter.

This is Yoko Suzuki.
She's a chef.

This is Alex Santos.
He's a personal trainer.

This is Gio Ferrari.
He's a student.
He's from Italy.

This is Liz Martin.
She's a Web designer
and singer.

This is Kim Davis.
She's David's co-worker.

The Video

Welcome to the *Touchstone* Video. In this video you will get to know six people who are friends: David, Liz, Yoko, Alex, Kim, and Gio. You can read about them on page iv.

You will also hear them use the English that you are studying in the *Touchstone* Student's Books. Each of the four levels of the Video breaks down as follows:

Episode 1	Act 1	*Student's Book units 1–3*
	Act 2	
	Act 3	

Episode 2	Act 1	*Student's Book units 4–6*
	Act 2	
	Act 3	

Episode 3	Act 1	*Student's Book units 7–9*
	Act 2	
	Act 3	

Episode 4	Act 1	*Student's Book units 10–12*
	Act 2	
	Act 3	

Explanation of the DVD Menu

To play one Episode of the Video:
- On the Main Menu, select *Episode Menu*.
- On the Episode Menu, select the appropriate *Play Episode*.

To play one Act of the Video:
- On the Main Menu, select *Episode Menu*.
- On the Episode Menu, select *Act Menu*.
- On the Act Menu, select the appropriate *Play Act*.

To play the Video with subtitles:
- On the Main Menu, Episode Menu, or Act Menu, select *Subtitles*.
- On the Subtitles Menu, select *Subtitles on*. The DVD will then automatically take you back to the menu you were on before.

To cancel the subtitles:
- On the Main Menu, Episode Menu, or Act Menu, select *Subtitles*.
- On the Subtitles Menu, select *Subtitles off*. The DVD will then automatically take you back to the menu you were on before.

The Worksheets

For each Act there are *Before you watch*, *While you watch*, and *After you watch* worksheets.

For *While you watch* worksheets:
- Find **DVD** [0] on your worksheet.
- Input this number on the Video menu using your remote control. The DVD will then play only the segment of the Video you need to watch to complete the task.

We hope you enjoy the *Touchstone* Video!

Episode 3 Out and About

Act 1

Before you watch

A Label the pictures with the words in the box.

blouse	boots	dress	jacket	✓jeans
pants	shoes	skirt	sweater	T-shirt

1. This is a
   _____ .

2. These are
   jeans_____ .

3. This is a
   _____ .

4. This is a
   _____ .

5. These are
   _____ .

6. This is a
   _____ .

7. This is a
   _____ .

8. This is a
   _____ .

9. These are
   _____ .

10. These are
    _____ .

B Choose the correct form.

1. I'm sorry! I can't come to the party because I **want to** / **have to** stay home and study.
2. We don't have any more food. We **like to** / **need to** go to the supermarket.
3. The teacher said we **have to** / **want to** take a test next week.
4. Do you **need to** / **want to** see a movie tonight? Let's go to the Roxie.
5. I **like to** / **want to** run when I have time. What do you do for exercise?
6. Sorry, I've got to go. I **have to** / **like to** meet someone at four.
7. You look great! You don't **like to** / **need to** lose weight.
8. What do you **have to** / **like to** do in your free time? Do you play sports?

While you watch

A Does Yoko like Liz's outfits? Check (✓) yes or no. Then answer the question.

1. ☐ Yes ☐ No

2. ☐ Yes ☐ No

3. ☐ Yes ☐ No

4. ☐ Yes ☐ No

5. ☐ Yes ☐ No

6. ☐ Yes ☐ No

7. What does Liz buy? _____

B Circle the correct answers.

1. Liz **wants to** / **doesn't want to** wear something different.
2. Liz **wants to** / **doesn't want to** wear a dress.
3. Liz **likes** / **doesn't like** the skirt and boots.
4. Liz **needs to** / **doesn't need to** buy a new outfit.
5. Liz **likes to** / **doesn't like to** go shopping.
6. Yoko **has to** / **doesn't have to** meet a friend later.

While you watch

DVD [34]
VHS 22:14
−24:00

C What do Liz and Yoko say about these items? Match the items with the comments. (There are two answers for one of the items.)

1. jeans and a T-shirt ____
2. the dress ____
3. the high heels ____
4. the skirt ____
5. the boots ____

a. a bad idea
b. fun
c. dressy
d. comfortable
e. old
f. uncomfortable

DVD [35]
VHS 24:26
−27:28

D Listen for these sentences. Circle the correct answers.

1. Definitely. That looks ____ .
   a. wonderful   b. nice
2. Well, let's compare prices. How much ____ ?
   a. are they   b. do they cost
3. The skirt is, wow, ____ dollars.
   a. 58   b. 68
4. Oh! It's on sale. ____ percent off!
   a. 15   b. 50
5. And the sweater . . . oh, no! It's ____ dollars!
   a. 75   b. 79

6. You look ____ . I like both outfits.
   a. great   b. comfortable
7. You're wearing your ____ clothes!
   a. old   b. new
8. I'm just ____ in jeans and a T-shirt.
   a. happy   b. comfortable
9. It's a little ____ , right?
   a. special   b. different

After you watch

A What do Liz and Yoko say about each of the items?
Match the items with the comments.

1. the jeans and T-shirt __b__   a. It's very special!
2. the high heels _____   b. They're comfortable.
3. the skirt _____   c. They're uncomfortable.
4. the sweater _____   d. It's really old, but fun!
5. the jacket _____   e. It's expensive.

B What can you remember about the story?
Tell a partner.

*"Liz usually wears jeans and a T-shirt because they're comfortable.
But she wants to wear something different tonight because she's singing at the café."*

C Work with a partner. Complete the conversation. Circle the correct forms
and add your own ideas in the blanks. Then practice the conversation.

A I'm looking for a jacket. What do you think of (**this**) / **these**?
B Um, yeah. **It's** / **They're** OK.
A You don't like **it** / **them**.
B Not really. Um. . . .
A Maybe you're right. **It's** / **They're** a little _____ .
B Well, let's see. What about **this** / **these**?
A **That looks** / **Those look** _____ !

Role-play a similar conversation using other clothing items.

D Ask two classmates these questions, and write their answers. How are they
the same? How are they different?

	Name _____	*Name* _____
1. What do you usually wear to school or work?		
2. Do you like to wear dressy clothes?		
3. How often do you shop for clothes?		
4. Do you like shopping for clothes?		
5. What clothes do you buy a lot?		

Before you watch

A Label the picture with the words in the box.

| gym | museum | ✓café | park | restaurant |

1. café

2. _____

3. _____

4. _____

5. _____

B Match the places to the activities you can do there. Draw lines.
Compare answers with a partner.

You can . . .

have a picnic   at a movie theater.
buy stamps   at a gym.
watch a movie   at a post office.
eat pizza   at a museum.
see an art exhibit   in a park.
take yoga classes   at an Italian restaurant.

C Match the sentences with the responses. Then practice with a partner.

1. How are you doing? __b__
2. Are you enjoying the city? _____
3. Are you studying hard? _____
4. I have a part-time job. _____
5. I'm not feeling very well. _____

a. Yes, I am. I have a quiz tomorrow.
b. I'm OK. A little tired.
c. Oh, that's too bad.
d. Oh, yes. I love it here.
e. Really? What do you do?

While you watch

DVD 36
VHS 27:34
−30:52

A Check (✓) the topics that Liz and Gio discuss.

☐ Gio's school   ☐ things to do in the neighborhood
☐ Liz's work   ☐ going out for dinner
☐ Gio's family   ☐ going to the gym

DVD 37
VHS 27:34
−30:52

B Circle the correct answers. For some items, both *a* and *b* are correct.

1. Gio has _____ .
   a. difficult classes
   b. great teachers
2. Liz is _____ .
   a. very busy
   b. singing a lot
3. Gio doesn't _____ .
   a. know the neighborhood well
   b. go out a lot
4. Liz tells Gio about _____ .
   a. some restaurants
   b. a park

5. Tonight, Liz is _____ .
   a. going out for dinner
   b. singing at a café
6. Gio asks Liz about _____ food.
   a. Italian
   b. Mexican
7. Gio needs to leave the café to _____ .
   a. meet Alex
   b. go to a class

DVD 38
VHS 28:30
−30:52

C Who says these sentences? Check (✓) Gio or Liz. Then watch the video and check your answers.

	Gio	Liz
1. What can you do around here for fun?		
2. I love to be outside when the weather's nice.		
3. Do you want to have dinner sometime?		
4. I know the perfect place.		
5. How often do you go to the gym?		
6. It's, uh, kind of like yoga.		

DVD 39
VHS 28:30
–29:40

D **What can you do in the neighborhood for fun? Watch the video and check (✓) the things Liz says.**

☑ visit museums   ☐ go to the park

☐ eat Mexican food   ☐ hang out in cafés

☐ go shopping   ☐ visit historic sites

☐ take a walking tour   ☐ hear live music

DVD 40
VHS 27:34
–28:35

E **Listen and complete the conversation.**

Liz   Hi, Gio! Can I join you?

Gio   Oh, hi, Liz. Of course.

Liz   How are you? How's it (1) _____ ?

Gio   Everything's great, thanks!

Liz   What are you (2) _____ ?

Gio   Oh, it's for school. Business English.

Liz   How is school? Are you (3) _____ hard?

Gio   Yeah, I am. Uh, my classes are a little difficult, but I like them.

Liz   Well, that's cool!

Gio   How about you? How are you doing?

Liz   I'm OK. Well, I'm a little tired. I'm not (4) _____ a lot.

Gio   Oh, that's not good! Why? What's going on?

Liz   Well, I'm (5) _____ a lot, and I have my Web design job.

Gio   Yes, but that's part-time, right?

Liz   Yeah, but I'm just always busy.

Gio   Really? That's too bad.

Liz   So . . . uh, are you (6) _____ the city?

Gio   Oh, yeah! I like it here a lot.

After you watch

A What can you remember about Liz? Complete the sentences
in your own words.

Liz is tired because she works _____ and she _____ .
In her free time, she likes to _____ .

B Work with a partner. Look at the scene. Write what Gio could say.
Then practice the conversation.

Liz Hi, Gio! Can I join you?

Gio Oh, hi, Liz. <u>Yes, please. / Of course.</u>

Liz How's it going?

Gio _____

How are *you* doing?

Liz _____

So, are you enjoying the city?

Gio _____

Liz Are you going out a lot?

Gio _____

What can you do around here for fun?

Liz Oh, you can do a lot. _____

_____

Gio Sounds fun!

C Where can you do the following in your city or town? Write sentences.
Compare your answers with a partner.

eat outdoors	go to a show	have Italian food
hear live music	study English	take exercise classes

1. _____

2. _____

3. _____

4. _____

5. _____

6. _____

Act 3

Before you watch

A Complete the sentences with the words in the box.

doing laundry	working out	✓ singing	studying	working

1. They're <u>singing</u> .   2. She's _____ .   3. He's _____ .

4. They're _____ .   5. He's _____ .

B Number the lines of the conversation in the correct order. Then practice with a partner.

_____ Nothing. The tickets are free.

_____ Yes, it is. It starts at 7:00. Let's meet at 6:30.

__2__ Yes, I am. Why?

_____ Oh, great! See you tomorrow.

_____ Oh, yes, I do. I love plays! Is it a comedy?

__1__ Are you free tomorrow evening?

_____ OK. How much does it cost?

_____ Well, I have tickets to that new play at the Vincent Theater. Do you want to go?

While you watch

DVD [41]
VHS 30:58
−34:45

A Number the scenes in the correct order.

a. ____

b. _1_

c. ____

d. ____

e. ____

DVD [42]
VHS 30:58
−34:45

B Check (✓) true or false. Then try to correct the false sentences.

1. David is seeing a concert tonight. ☐ True ☐ False
_____

2. It starts at 8:30. ☐ True ☐ False
_____

3. Alex is working out at the gym. ☐ True ☐ False
_____

4. David leaves Yoko a message. ☐ True ☐ False
_____

5. Liz wants to see *The Perfect Day* sometime. ☐ True ☐ False
_____

6. David tells Liz, "Good luck tomorrow." ☐ True ☐ False
_____

7. Gio has three big exams tomorrow. ☐ True ☐ False
_____

8. Alex leaves David a message. ☐ True ☐ False
_____

9. Kim takes the extra ticket. ☐ True ☐ False
_____

While you watch

C Why can't these people go to the play with David? Write the reasons. Then watch the video and check your answers.

DVD 43
VHS 30:58
−34:45

	Reason
1. Tom	
2. Liz	
3. Yoko	
4. Gio	
5. Alex	

D How do the conversations end? Watch the video and circle the correct answers.

DVD 44
VHS 30:58
−31:57

1.   *Alex* I'm just finishing my workout now.
       Can you call me / Can I call you back
       in five minutes?
  David Uh, **OK / no problem**. Sure.
       Talk to you **later / soon**.

DVD 45
VHS 32:25
−33:29

2. *David* Oh, well. Uh, listen, Liz. I have to
       go / leave. I have to find someone for
       this ticket.
    Liz Of course. Call me **later / tomorrow**, OK?
 David OK! Oh, and good luck tonight!
    Liz Thanks. **Bye / Good-bye**!

E Complete the two phone messages.

DVD 46
VHS 31:58
−32:24

  David (1) ____Hi____ , Kim. It's David. I have a (2) _____ ticket to see
       The Perfect Day. It's at the Grand (3) _____ . Uh, it
       (4) _____ in half an hour. Can you come? (5) _____ me
       back! Bye.

DVD 47
VHS 34:04
−34:25

    Alex (6) _____ , David. It's Alex. Listen, I don't think I can go. I really
       (7) _____ to do my laundry tonight, and I (8) _____ to get up
       early tomorrow morning. I'm really (9) _____ . Anyway, have
       fun.

After you watch

A What can you remember? What is each person doing tonight?

1. Alex _____
2. Liz _____
3. Gio _____
4. Yoko _____

B Complete the conversations with the questions in the box.
Then practice with a partner.

> How much does it cost?
> What time does the concert start?
> Are you free tonight?

A Hi, Leo. (1) _____

B Yes, I am. Why?

A I have tickets to a concert. Jilly Cain is singing at
   the Coffee Stop.

B Oh, I love Jilly Cain! (2) _____
   _____

A 8:00.

B OK. (3) _____

A Nothing. I have free tickets. Jilly is a friend.

B Really? That's great! Let's meet at 7:30.

A OK, see you then.

C Ask two classmates these questions and write their answers. How are they
the same? How are they different?

	Name _____	Name _____
1. How often do you go to plays?		
2. How often do you go to movies?		
3. What kind of movies do you like?		
4. How often do you go to concerts?		
5. What kind of music do you like?		
6. Who is your favorite singer?		

Episode 4 Dinner Is Served

Act 1

Before you watch

A Match the simple present verbs with the simple past verbs in the box.

a. fell	c. finished	e. sent	g. went	i. walked	k. sang
b. had	d. was / were	f. did	h. wrote	j. worked	l. studied

1. have __b__
2. be ____
3. work ____
4. do ____
5. study ____
6. fall ____
7. write ____
8. send ____
9. walk ____
10. finish ____
11. go ____
12. sing ____

B What did Josh do yesterday? Write sentences under the pictures. Use the verbs and verb phrases in the box.

fell asleep	finished work	had dinner	met friends
✓ studied	walked in the park	went home	worked

Josh had a busy day yesterday. . . .

1. <u>He studied.</u>
2. _____
3. _____
4. _____

5. _____
6. _____
7. _____
8. _____

C Match the questions and answers. Then practice with a partner.

1. Are you OK? You look tired. __d__
2. What did you do last night? ____
3. How did your exams go? ____
4. How are you? ____
5. How was the restaurant? ____

a. It was great. The food was delicious, and the service was excellent.
b. Fine. I had a fun week.
c. OK. I think I did well.
d. I am. I'm exhausted. I studied all night.
e. I went out with friends.

DVD 48
VHS 34:50
−39:28

A Watch the video and check (✓) true or false. Then try to correct the false sentences.

1. Yoko went out with her friends last night.   ☐ True ☐ False

_____

2. Liz had lunch with Gio.   ☐ True ☐ False

_____

3. Liz and Gio were both tired.   ☐ True ☐ False

_____

4. Gio fell asleep during dinner.   ☐ True ☐ False

_____

5. Yoko tells an embarrassing story.   ☐ True ☐ False

_____

6. Yoko's story is about a telephone call.   ☐ True ☐ False

_____

7. Liz and Yoko decide to go out for dinner.   ☐ True ☐ False

_____

DVD 49
VHS 34:50
−39:28

B Listen for these sentences. Match the sentences and the responses.

1. I was exhausted by the end of the night. __d__
2. Actually, I had dinner with Gio. _____
3. Oh, I'm sorry. _____
4. Well, I guess I slept for two hours, maybe. _____
5. . . . I think I did really well. I'm surprised. _____
6. Liz? Liz, are you OK? _____
7. After dinner, we just came home. _____
8. I remember one time I did something really embarrassing. _____
9. But I sent the e-mail to Peter by mistake! _____
10. We can cook! _____

a. You poor thing! Why?
b. You did?!
c. You know what? That's not so bad.
d. I bet.
e. Oh, Yoko, that's a great idea.
f. Well, good for you!
g. Really?! You did?!
h. Are you OK, Gio?
i. Really? What?
j. Oh. Sorry! I-I'm OK.

While you watch

DVD 50
VHS 35:20
−37:24

C Circle the correct answers.

1. Liz met Gio _____ .
   a. at his school
   b. in the park
2. There are a lot of _____ dishes on the menu.
   a. fish
   b. pasta
3. Gio thinks he _____ on his exams.
   a. did well
   b. didn't do well
4. Liz _____ at the Park Café last night.
   a. worked
   b. sang
5. Liz had _____ at the café last night.
   a. a great time
   b. an awful time

D Complete the two stories.

DVD 51
VHS 37:24
−37:45

Liz's story

So we were both tired, but it was (1) _____ !
I mean, the restaurant had a (2) _____
atmosphere, the food was (3) _____ ,
and the service was really (4) _____ .
Gio and I talked about a lot of things. And we
(5) _____ a lot. I even learned some
Italian words.

DVD 52
VHS 38:28
−39:00

Yoko's story

I (6) _____ a horrible e-mail to the wrong
person. I (7) _____ (8) _____ at my friend
Peter, and I (9) _____ to my friend Sarah
about it. But I sent the e-mail to Peter by
(10) _____ !

After you watch

A What can you remember? Make a list of what Liz and Gio did together.

They met after Liz finished work. They _____

_____

_____

_____

B Change the verbs to the past tense. Then work in pairs. Take turns saying what you did yesterday, last night, and last weekend. Use the verbs and your own ideas.

1. finish _____
2. go out _____
3. have _____
4. laugh _____
5. meet _____
6. see _____

7. send _____
8. sleep _____
9. study _____
10. walk _____
11. work _____

C Think of a day when you were really busy. Tell a partner about your day. Use the sentences to help you.

1. It was (*when*).
2. I was really busy because (*reason*).
3. I went to bed at (*time*).
4. I got up at (*time*).
5. I (*list activities*) all day.
6. By the end of the day, I was (*feeling*).

Act 2

Before you watch

Complete the crossword puzzle with the foods in the box.

| beans | cheese | garlic | meat | onions | pasta | peppers | rice | shrimp | tomatoes |

Across

Down

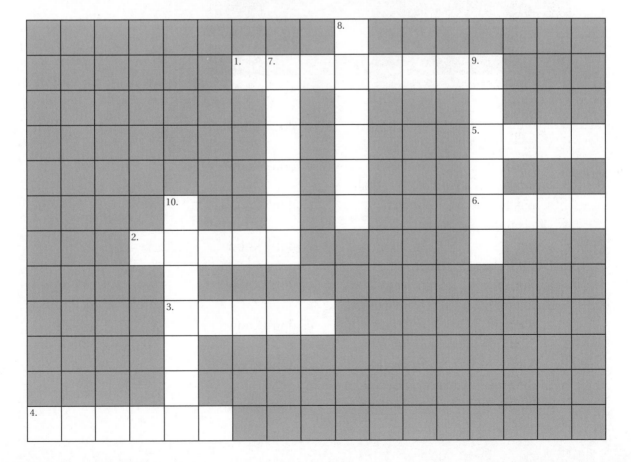

While you watch

DVD 53
VHS 39:35
−43:45

A Match the people to their eating preferences.

| Liz | Alex | Gio | David | Kim |

1. Liz _____   a. can't eat anything hot.
2. Alex _____   b. doesn't want pasta.
3. Gio _____   c. eats everything.
4. David _____   d. is a vegetarian.
5. Kim _____   e. is allergic to shellfish.

DVD 54
VHS 39:35
−43:45

B Circle the correct answers. Circle *c. don't know* if the answer is not given.

1. Dinner is at _____ .
   a. 6:00   b. 7:00   c. don't know
2. Yoko suggests a spicy _____ dish.
   a. chicken   b. bean   c. don't know
3. Jambalaya is a kind of _____ dish.
   a. pasta   b. rice   c. don't know
4. Gio is not a _____ eater.
   a. big   b. picky   c. don't know
5. Goulash has _____ in it.
   a. meat   b. eggs   c. don't know
6. Yoko and Liz need _____ cheese.
   a. a lot of   b. some   c. don't know
7. _____ wants to bring a friend.
   a. Alex   b. David   c. don't know
8. In the end, Yoko and Liz decide to make _____ .
   a. jambalaya   b. goulash   c. don't know

DVD 55
VHS 40:45
−42:33

C Watch the video. What do you hear?

1. What does Yoko put in jambalaya? Cross out the incorrect word(s).
   rice   fish   tomatoes
   carrots   onions   shrimp

2. What does Yoko put in goulash? Cross out the incorrect word(s).
   hamburger meat   cheese   tomatoes   shrimp
   onions   garlic   pasta   peppers

DVD 56
VHS 39:35
−42:33

D What do Yoko and Liz have? Circle the correct answers.

They have . . . .

1. **some / a lot of** pasta   6. **some / a lot of** hamburger meat
2. **no / a lot of** beans   7. **no / some** shrimp
3. **some / a lot of** tomatoes   8. **no / a lot of** garlic
4. **no / some** green peppers   9. **no / some** cheese
5. **one / two** onion(s)

E Complete the conversations.

DVD 57
VHS 40:38
−41:12

  Liz Let's see. We have some tomatoes. And some green peppers.
Yoko Do we (1) _____ (2) _____ onions?
  Liz We have one.
Yoko Hmm. Do we (3) _____ (4) _____ meat in the freezer?
  Liz Um, there's some hamburger meat and . . . some shrimp.

DVD 58
VHS 42:00
−42:33

Yoko OK. Perfect. Let's start a list. (5) _____ (6) _____ onions do we have?
  Liz Just one.
Yoko Well, we need two. Now, do we (7) _____ (8) _____ garlic?
  Liz No, I don't see any.
Yoko Need garlic. . . . OK.
  Liz Um. . . . I don't see any cheese. Do we (9) _____ (10) _____ ?
Yoko Oh, yeah.
  Liz OK. (11) _____ (12) _____ cheese do we need?
Yoko Just a minute.

After you watch

A Describe the problem that Liz and Yoko have. What do you think they could make for dinner? Then play the beginning of Act 3 to find out what they made.

"I think they could make . . ."

B Look at the picture. Complete the sentences with the words in the box.

a lot of	any	are	aren't	✓is	isn't	some	some

1. There <u>is</u> a lot of rice.
2. There _____ any cheese.
3. There are _____ beans.
4. There's _____ pasta.
5. There _____ any tomatoes.
6. There's _____ meat.
7. There _____ three green peppers.
8. There isn't _____ garlic.

C Write some sentences about the food you have at home. Then compare with a partner.

_____

_____

_____

_____

D Add two questions about eating habits to the chart. Then ask two classmates the questions and write their answers. How are they the same? How are they different?

	Name _____	Name _____
1. How many cups of coffee or tea do you drink every day?		
2. How much water do you drink every day?		
3. What do you usually eat for lunch?		
4. What do you usually drink with meals?		
5.		
6.		

Episode 4 Dinner Is Served

Act 3

Before you watch

A Label the pictures with the words in the box.

| camping | hiking | shopping | ✓snorkeling | windsurfing |

1. <u>snorkeling</u>

2. _____

3. _____

4. _____

5. _____

B Unscramble the words. Complete each sentence.

1. That movie was very good. It was <u>excellent</u> ! (TENELCELX)
2. The food was very good. It was <u>d</u>_____ ! (SLUICOIED)
3. The people in that house always say hello. They're very <u>f</u>_____ . (LIFRENDY)
4. I'm very hungry. I'm <u>s</u>_____ ! (GRISTNAV)
5. You're going to Africa for two weeks! How <u>e</u>_____ ! (TIXEGINC)
6. You only sleep four hours every night! That's <u>a</u>_____ ! (ZIGANAM)

C Match each beginning with two endings.

1. I got <u>a</u> ____
2. Susan went ____ ____
3. Kevin took ____ ____
4. We had ____ ____

    a. a new camera last year.
    b. a party on Saturday.
    c. a tour around the city.
    d. camping last weekend.
    e. lost in the mountains.
    f. on vacation to Mexico.
    g. rice and beans for dinner.
    h. some photos of the trip.

While you watch

DVD 59
VHS 43:51
−47:18

A Circle all the correct answers. (One, two, or three answers are possible.)

1. What did the friends eat for dinner?
   a. hamburgers   b. rice and beans   c. grilled vegetables

2. What does David talk about?
   a. the meal   b. the service   c. the prices

3. What did Kim get on vacation?
   a. a necklace   b. a camera   c. a hat

4. Where did Kim go?
   a. England   b. Australia   c. Mexico

5. What do we see in the first two pictures?
   a. the Opera House   b. the Harbor Bridge   c. Sydney Harbor

6. What mountains does Kim visit?
   a. the Green Mountains   b. the Blue Mountains   c. the Red Mountains

7. What was Kim's favorite part of her trip?
   a. the outback   b. the mountains   c. the beach

8. What animals do they talk about?
   a. kangaroos   b. koala bears   c. dolphins

9. What does Gio want to do?
   a. apologize   b. make dinner for Liz   c. take Liz and Yoko
                            and Yoko   to dinner

While you watch

DVD 60
VHS 44:17
−46:46

B Here are some pictures of Kim's trip. Put them in the correct order.

a. snorkeling _____

b. windsurfing _____

c. camping _____

d. kangaroos _____

e. the mountains _____

f. shopping _____

DVD 61
VHS 44:17
−46:46

C Check (✓) where Kim did each activity.

	Sydney	*The Outback*	*The Blue Mountains*
1. went windsurfing			
2. went hiking			
3. took a tour			
4. went camping			
5. saw wildlife			
6. went shopping			

DVD 62
VHS 44:17
−46:15

D Match the questions and the answers. Then watch the video.
Listen for the questions and complete the answers.

1. How long were you there? _____
2. Do you have any pictures? _____
3. Did you like windsurfing? _____
4. What was that like? _____
5. Um, what is the outback? _____
6. What was the weather like? _c_

a. You know, it was _____ at first, but
   now I think I'm pretty _____ at it.
b. About _____ weeks.
c. It was hot, but not too _____ .
d. Actually, I got a new _____ before I left.
   I have some pictures _____ .
e. It was _____ .
f. Um, it's outside of the _____ . It's like a desert.

After you watch

A What can you remember? Work with a partner. Describe Kim's trip in as much detail as possible.

"Kim went to Australia for three weeks. She . . ."

B Imagine that you have just come back from an interesting trip. Make some notes in the chart.

Where did you go?	Who went with you?	How long was your trip?

What did you do?	How was the weather?	What was the best part?

Work with a partner. Have a conversation about your trip.

Where did you go?

Well, we . . .

That's exciting! How long were you there?

We spent a week in . . .

What was it like?

It was beautiful / amazing / wonderful.

Did you see . . . ?

We didn't . . . but we . . .

Illustration credits

Dominic Bugatto: 9
Chuck Gonzales: 13, 37, 45
Frank Montagna: 5, 16, 25, 40
Phil Williams: 4

Photography credits

1 (*top row, left to right*) ©Shutterstock; ©Shutterstock; ©Alamy; ©Shutterstock; ©Jupiter Images; (*bottom row, left to right*) ©Jupiter Images; ©Courtesy of Jamey O'Quinn; ©Photos.com; ©Punchstock; ©Shutterstock

5 (*left to right*) ©Jupiter Images; ©Jupiter Images; ©Alamy; ©Alamy

10 (*top to bottom*) ©Alamy; ©Photos.com

12 (*left to right*) ©Photos.com; ©Photos.com; ©Alamy

17 (*top row, left to right*) ©Alamy; ©Kim Karpeles/Alamy; ©Alamy; ©Alamy; (*bottom row, left to right*) ©Mark Scheuern/Alamy; ©Punchstock; ©Kevin Foy/Alamy; ©Jupiter Images

20 ©Alamy

21 (*left to right*) ©Lon C. Diehl/Photo Edit; ©David Young-Wolff/Photo Edit

24 ©Jupiter Images

29 (*top row, left to right*) ©Jupiter Images; ©Jupiter Images; ©Shutterstock; (*bottom row, left to right*) ©Alamy; ©Shutterstock

33 (*top row, left to right*) ©Jupiter Images; ©Corbis; ©Corbis; (*bottom row, both*) ©Corbis

36 (*top to bottom*) ©Alamy; ©Jupiter Images

41 (*top row, left to right*) ©Alamy; ©Jupiter Images; ©Punchstock; ©Getty Images; ©Jupiter Images; ©Jupiter Images; (*bottom row, left to right*) ©Alamy; ©Alamy; ©Jupiter Images; ©Jupiter Images

47 (*top row, left to right*) ©David Smith/Image by Interface; ©Jupiter Images; ©DW Stock Picture Library; (*bottom row, left to right*) ©Corbis; ©Punchstock; ©Alamy

48 (*left to right*) ©Jupiter Images; ©Punchstock

Irregular verbs

Base form	Simple past
be	was / were
become	became
begin	began
break	broke
bring	brought
build	built
buy	bought
catch	caught
choose	chose
come	came
cost	cost
cut	cut
do	did
draw	drew
drink	drank
drive	drove
eat	ate
fall	fell
feel	felt
find	found
forget	forgot
get	got
give	gave
go	went
grow	grew
have	had
hear	heard
hit	hit
hold	held
hurt	hurt
keep	kept
know	knew
leave	left
lend	lent

Base form	Simple past
lie	lay
lose	lost
make	made
mean	meant
meet	met
pay	paid
put	put
read	read
ride	rode
ring	rang
run	ran
say	said
see	saw
sell	sold
send	sent
shut	shut
sing	sang
sit	sat
sleep	slept
speak	spoke
spend	spent
stand	stood
steal	stole
swim	swam
take	took
teach	taught
tell	told
think	thought
throw	threw
understand	understood
wear	wore
win	won
write	wrote